"Lynne Finch has a simple way of stating the complex and making perfect sense at the same time. *Taking Your First Shot* is about more than just hitting the target, it takes you through many first steps toward safe and effective handgun-related necessities women must master when personal protection is paramount. This book is written for real women in the real world, in an easy to read format ladies can enjoy!"

—Susan Carrichner Rexrode,
Founder, Shooting for Women Alliance

"Lynne's journey from shooter, to defensive shooting student to teacher sharing her experience and knowledge has been a thorough one. She has a great deal to offer the new shooter, especially the woman new to defensive handguns, and does a great job of communicating important lessons in *Taking Your First Shot*."

—Rob Pincus, I.C.E. Training Company

"This book is easy and enjoyable to read, addressing issues that have been overlooked in other books. Since very few new shooters have been raised in a shooting family, they didn't have anyone to guide them through their first gun purchase, teach them how to see if the gun fits their hand, or guide them in gun store etiquette—until this book came along. Along with the requisite safety information and basics of gun ownership, this book provides self defense information that both women and men will find useful. Lynne's writing style is both informative and conversational, it feels as though she's taking you into her confidences and sharing secrets that the 'good ole boys' used to keep to themselves."

—C. S. Wilson, co-founder TheGunDivas.com

"*Taking Your First Shot* is a great introduction for women seeking more information on Personal Safety and women that are looking to begin on their path as a Defensive Shooter. Male and Female Instructors alike can learn a wealth of information from this fun, witty and entertaining approach to women's safety!"

—Evan Carson, President & Chief Instructor,
Innovative Defensive Solutions, LLC

"Excellent book! A must read for new shooters. As a firearms instructor and blogger I am constantly asked which books I recommend for someone just learning about guns and self defense. In addition to Massad Ayoob's *In The Gravest Extreme* and Kathy Jackson's *The Cornered Cat: A Woman's Guide to Concealed Carry*, I will now also be strongly suggesting *Taking Your First Shot.*"

—A Girl, agirlandhergun.com

TAKING YOUR FIRST SHOT

A WOMAN'S INTRODUCTION TO DEFENSIVE
SHOOTING AND PERSONAL SAFETY

Lynne Finch

Photography by **Dr. Russ Charlesworth Jr.**

Skyhorse Publishing

Skyhorse Publishing books may be purchased in bulk at special discounts for sales promotion, corporate gifts, fund-raising, or educational purposes. Special editions can also be created to specifications. For details, contact the Special Sales Department, Skyhorse Publishing, 307 West 36th Street, 11th Floor, New York, NY 10018 or info@skyhorsepublishing.com.

Skyhorse® and Skyhorse Publishing® are registered trademarks of Skyhorse Publishing, Inc. ®, a Delaware corporation.

www.skyhorsepublishing.com

10 9 8 7 6 5 4 3 2 1

Library of Congress Cataloging-in-Publication Data is available on file.

ISBN: 978-1- 62087-717-3

Printed in China

DISCLAIMER

Check your state and local laws before carrying a handgun, concealed or otherwise. Laws vary widely from state to state. Some states allow concealed carry without a permit, some require a permit, and some states do not allow concealed handgun carry at all. All states put restrictions on where and how handguns can be carried legally. In addition, several states outlaw particular modes of concealed carry. Your local law enforcement department or district attorney's office should know the details.
This book is not designed to take the place of a qualified and competent instructor; rather, it is a resource designed to supplement quality training.

Dedicated to the memory of Rosalie "Terri" Matthews, a special friend who helped me find the courage to take my "first shot."

TABLE OF CONTENTS ───

Foreword   **XIII**

Preface   **XIX**

Acknowledgments   **XXI**

Chapter 1   WELCOME TO THE WORLD OF SHOOTING   **1**

Chapter 2   FINDING AN INSTRUCTOR   **6**

Chapter 3   YOUR FIRST TRIP TO THE RANGE   **12**

Chapter 4   CYLINDERS, SLIDES, AND ACTIONS...OH MY!   **17**

Chapter 5   NAME THAT PART!   **19**

Chapter 6   BUYING YOUR FIRST GUN   **21**

Chapter 7   SHOOTING FUNDAMENTALS   **34**

Chapter 8   MALFUNCTIONS   **48**

Chapter 9   PRACTICE, PRACTICE, PRACTICE   **53**

Chapter 10   CLEANING YOUR GUN   **64**

Chapter 11   STORING AND CARING FOR YOUR GUN   **69**

Chapter 12   PRACTICE VERSUS DEFENSIVE AMMUNITION   **71**

Chapter 13   NEXT STEPS   **74**

Chapter 14   PHYSICAL LIMITATIONS DON'T HAVE
                 TO STOP YOU FROM SHOOTING   **76**

Chapter 15   SITUATIONAL AWARENESS   **79**

Chapter 16   BASICS OF UNARMED PERSONAL DEFENSE   **87**

Chapter 17   MAKING THE DECISION TO CARRY
                 A CONCEALED FIREARM   **107**

Chapter 18   HOLSTERS AND DRESSING TO CARRY
CONCEALED   **111**

Chapter 19   INSIDE OR OUTSIDE   **124**

Chapter 20   PROPORTIONAL RESPONSE   **129**

Chapter 21   PRACTICE VERSUS DEFENSIVE SHOOTING   **131**

Chapter 22   IF ONLY   **133**

Chapter 23   NATIONAL TAKE YOUR DAUGHTER
TO THE RANGE DAY   **135**

Glossary of Terms   **137**

About the Author   **147**

TABLE OF FIGURES ————

Figure 1-1.   ANNIE OAKLEY   2

Figure 1-2.   RUGER LCP WITH LASERMAX   5

Figure 2-1.   STUDENTS TAKING NOTES IN A CLASS   7

Figure 2-2.   INSTRUCTOR AND STUDENT
ON THE RANGE   10

Figure 3-1.   STUDENT IN PROPER ATTIRE AND SAFETY
EQUIPMENT   13

Figure 3-2.   EYES AND EARS   16

Figure 4-1.   THIS SMITH & WESSON BODYGUARD 38 IS AN
EXAMPLE OF A DOUBLE ACTION REVOLVER   18

Figure 5-1.   RUGER SP101 - REVOLVER   19

Figure 5-2.   GLOCK 19 - 9MM SEMI-AUTOMATIC   20

Figure 5-3.   RUGER P95 - SEMI-AUTOMATIC   20

Figure 6-1.   KEL-TEC P-3AT   22

Figure 6-2.   CHARTER ARMS PINK LADY OFF-DUTY   23

Figure 6-3.   RACKING THE SLIDE   26

Figure 6-4.   GRIP MASTER   27

Figure 6-5.   STRONG HAND, BACK STRAP TO TRIGGER   28

Figure 6-6.   BROWNING BUCKMARK - .22 TARGET
PISTOL WITH NON-STOCK ACCESSORIES   30

Figure 6-7.   BASIC CLEANING KIT   32

Figure 6-8.   GLOCK 19 – GLORY, GRACE, AND
GLINDA THE GOOD GLOCK   33

Figure 7-1.   SHOOTING STANCE SHOWN FROM ABOVE   35

Figure 7-2.   SHOOTING STANCE SHOWN FROM SIDE   36

Figure 7-3.   DOMINANT EYE EXERCISE   36

Figure 7-4.   STRONG HAND PICKING UP PISTOL   38

Figure 7-5.   TWO HAND SEMI-AUTOMATIC GRIP   38

Figure 7-6.   TWO HAND REVOLVER GRIP   39

Figure 7-7.   LOADING THE MAGAZINE   40

Figure 7-8.   IN YOUR WORK SPACE   41

Figure 7-9.   WHY YOU OPERATE IN YOUR WORK SPACE   41

Figure 7-10.   INDEXING THE MAGAZINE   42

Figure 7-11.   RACKING THE SLIDE   42

Figure 7-12.   CLEAR AND LOCKED BACK
                  SEMI-AUTOMATIC   43

Figure 7-13.   LOADING A REVOLVER   44

Figure 7-14.   UNLOADING A REVOLVER   44

Figure 7-15.   PERFECT SIGHT PICTURE   45

Figure 7-16.   FINGER ON THE TRIGGER   46

Figure 8-1.   TAP, RACK, REACQUIRE   50

Figure 8-2.   SEMI-AUTOMATIC RECOIL SPRING   51

Figure 8-3.   STOVE PIPE MALFUNCTION   52

Figure 9-1.   DUMMY ROUNDS   54

Figure 9-2.   SHOOTING AROUND A BARRIER   57

Figure 9-3.   LOW READY POSITION   59

Figure 9-4.   REHOLSTERING   60

Figure 9-5.   SCANNING FOR DANGER   60

Figure 9-6.   INSERTING A FRESH MAGAZINE
                  (RELOADING)   61

Figure 9-7.	GLOCK 19 BLUE GUN AND REAL PISTOL	62
Figure 10-1.	CLEANING THE BORE	66
Figure 10-2.	REMOVING THE RECOIL SPRING FOR CLEANING	67
Figure 10-3.	REASSEMBLING PISTOL	67
Figure 12-1.	REMINGTON 9MM PRACTICE ROUND, HORNADY 9MM CRITICAL DEFENSE HOLLOW POINT AND MAGTECH GUARDIAN GOLD HP 9MM	72
Figure 13-1.	DEFENSIVE SHOOTING STUDENT	75
Figure 14-1.	MY PINK HOGUE SLEEVE ON MY GLOCK	77
Figure 15-1.	USING REFLECTIVE SURFACES	82
Figure 15-2.	ATM WITH MIRRORS	83
Figure 15-3.	COOPER COLOR CODE CHART	84
Figure 15-4.	BEING AWARE OF YOUR SURROUNDINGS	86
Figure 16-1.	BASIC DEFENSIVE POSTURE	90
Figure 16-2.	GETTING OFF THE "X"	90
Figure 16-3.	SPLAYED FINGERS	94
Figure 16-4.	SPLAYED FINGERS EQUAL STRENGTH AND RESISTANCE	94
Figure 16-5.	INCOMING HAYMAKER	95
Figure 16-6.	DEFLECTING THE HAYMAKER	96
Figure 16-7.	NECK GRAB FROM BEHIND (NOTICE SHOULDERS)	97
Figure 16-8.	PART-1 BEAR HUG FROM BEHIND	97
Figure 16-8.	PART-2 BEAR HUG FROM BEHIND	98
Figure 16-8	PART-3 BEAR HUG FROM BEHIND	98
Figure 16-9.	ARMS AGAINST THE WALL	99
Figure 16-10.	FACE RAKE	99

Figure 16-11.   FOREARM TO NECK   100

Figure 16-12.   TURNING IN TO PUSH HIM OFF BALANCE   100

Figure 16-13.   DRIVING ASSAILANT TO THE GROUND   101

Figure 16-14.   ELBOW STRIKE TO JAW   102

Figure 16-15.   ELBOW STRIKE TO RIBS   102

Figure 16-16.   FOOT STOMP   103

Figure 16-17.   SHIN RAKE   103

Figure 16-18.   ON THE GROUND DEFENSIVE POSTURE   104

Figure 16-19.   ON THE GROUND SIDEWAYS
KICK TO THE SHIN   105

Figure 18-1.   SAMPLING FROM MY HOLSTER BAG   112

Figure 18-2.   HOLSTER SHOULD COVER THE TRIGGER
GUARD AND HOLD YOUR GUN   113

Figure 18-3.   DRAWING FROM A CONCEALED
CARRY PURSE   118

Figure 18-4.   CAN YOU SPOT THE FIREARMS?   120

Figure 18-5.   CAN YOU SPOT THE FIREARMS? PART II   121

Figure 23-1.   NATIONAL TAKE YOUR DAUGHTER
TO THE RANGE DAY LOGO   135

FOREWORD

We live in a golden age for female gun owners. The very existence of the book you're reading proves that. Like many books that have come before it, Taking Your First Shot provides a friendly, easy introduction to handgun ownership. Unlike most firearms books, this one was written by a woman, for women. Due to this, the book will likely reach a much wider audience than it would have reached just a few short years ago, and I hope it does.

When I started www.CorneredCat.com back in 2004, good information about concealed carry for women wasn't easy to find. There were plenty of websites about guns, but most of them seemed to be written for aggressive young men with military fantasies. With a few rare exceptions, the web was a depressing wasteland for a woman who wanted to know more about responsible firearms ownership and use. And as for finding female-specific details about concealed carry—forget it! That wasn't happening and so I decided to put something out there, to claim some small corner of the ocean where a woman could go to learn about firearms.

I didn't realize when I did it that I was actually jumping onto the crest of a gigantic wave. Things look very different online now than they did ten years ago. Today, you can easily find many firearms blogs intended for female audiences, and there are many female-friendly places within the online firearms community.

The National Shooting Sports Foundation (NSSF) tells us that over 73% of firearms retailers report an increase in their number of female customers in 2011, (the most recent year for which figures are available). That's not news to anyone who's been hanging around gun shops or visiting with other women, but it's good to hear.

According to a Gallup poll performed in October 2011, self-reported firearms ownership recently reached its highest level in America since 1993. In that poll, 43% of female respondents reported having a gun in their homes. Even more intriguing, at least 23% of American women own a firearm that belongs to them personally—not to another member of their household. While some social groups treat firearms ownership, especially female firearms ownership, as some kind of weird aberration, it's really not. Nearly a quarter of American women own guns of their own.

These bare numbers match verbal reports from friends within the gun sales industry. "It's not just the number of women we see in the store," says one anonymous gun seller in Washington state. "The remarkable thing we're seeing is that a lot more women are driving their own purchases. They are not just coming along because someone else is pushing them here. They're not only accepting gift guns from their husbands or boyfriends. They are doing their own shopping. This is where they want to be and what they want to be doing."

Handgun ownership, too, has swung sharply upward in recent years. According to the NSSF, approximately 9 million people, or 3.8% of American adults, have active concealed carry permits. The demand for good information about handgun ownership and use is thus stronger than it has been at any other point during the past several years.

Finally, gun ownership as a whole is on the rise. Information from the National Criminal Instant Check System (NICS) tells us that more than twice as many background checks were performed in January 2013 than were done in the same month just three years earlier. In January 2000, NICS ran more than 639,000 checks for clear backgrounds to allow gun purchases. But by the end of that decade, the number regularly topped well over one million background checks every single month.

Taken together, all those numbers mean that we have a lot of people buying a lot of guns, and that many of those people are women. Large numbers of people are getting their concealed carry permits and learning how to shoot handguns. And we have a surprisingly strong surge of women moving into these traditionally "male" areas.

Why are so many women buying handguns and learning how to use them? Several reasons come to mind:

Shooting is fun. As many women have known throughout the years, target shooting provides excellent opportunities for enjoyment and relaxation in a friendly atmosphere. Not long ago, I stood next to a woman as she handled a gun for the very first time. She was nervous at first, but after she fired her first shot she turned around with a huge grin on her face. "Now that's a gun!" she exclaimed. "I can't believe how much fun that is!" Like many new shooters, she enjoyed taking her target home at the end of the day, because it reminded her of a pleasant memory.

Shooting provides a competitive outlet. Some people enjoy a contemplative, high-focus challenge such as long-range shooting at small targets. Others find their fun in fast events with lots of action. Want to dress up like an old-fashioned cowgirl? Get down and dirty in the prone shooting position? Shoot at falling steel plates, or swinging targets? Whatever flavor of shooting you prefer, there's probably a competition event centered around it.

Shooting is inclusive. Did you know that the oldest Olympic competitor was a shooter? Oscar Swahn of Sweden was over 72 years old when he competed at the 1920 Olympics. But some of the youngest Olympians also competed in shooting sports. Kim Rhode, who recently became the first American athlete to win an individual medal in five consecutive Olympics, was just 13 years old when she won the world championship in American skeet shooting, and only 17 years old when she became the youngest female Olympic gold medal winner in a shooting sport. Everyone, young or old, male or female, can enjoy shooting together and often compete on an even footing. There aren't many sports where that is true.

Shooting is social. Like many other hobbies and sports, shooting provides wonderful opportunities for like-minded people to meet and mingle. Julianna Crowder, founder of A Girl and A Gun Women's Shooting League, talks about this on her blog: "A Girl and A Gun Women's Shooting League has connected me with hundreds of women, all different stages of life and reasons for participating in shooting activities. No matter if it is a woman I meet in person at the range, or the gal I meet on Facebook across the country, we are all bonding in a sisterhood, the common interest of shooting guns because it is fun and we can invoke our own style." There are similar groups and clubs all over the country, and all serve the common purpose of meeting social needs while having fun.

Shooting is challenging. A friend of mine—who shall remain anonymous here!—tells the story of the first time she went to the range. She says, "I was super excited! When the range officer asked for my preference in targets, I replied that it didn't matter, because I would be turning it around anyway." Turning it around? Why, yes. She wanted to shoot a happy face on a blank piece of paper at long distance, just like she saw the actor do in *Lethal Weapon*. Then she adds: "It turns out that sometimes.... just sometimes... something that looks easy on TV may not actually be easy in real life."

Shooting helps you protect yourself. Although not all shooters go on to learn how to use their guns in self-defense, many do. The firearm meets a unique need in the self-defense world, one that can be filled with no other tool. It helps a middle-aged mom protect herself from a supremely fit, aggressive young man. It allows the senior citizens to defend herself against predation from people who are younger, faster, and more physically tough than she will ever be again. And unlike many other self-defense options, firearms allow the user to protect herself from a distance—improving the odds that she will go home unscathed to the people she loves.

Shooting builds the future. Not long after Lynne Finch founded National Take Your Daughters to the Range Day, she said something that really connected with me on this subject. She said, "Learning to shoot gives young women confidence, helps to build self-esteem, and introduces them to a sport they can participate in their whole lives." This is true on so many levels. Teaching a child to shoot builds social connections, improves confidence, fosters responsible decision-making, and encourages self-control. It also creates a bridge that reaches from the past to the future, linking the generations in an ongoing tradition.

That's why I'm glad to introduce this book by Lynne Finch, who has worked so hard to explain how firearms work and teach newcomers how to use them safely. She's an enthusiastic learner and an eager instructor, and I look forward to seeing more work from her in years to come.

Kathy Jackson
Author of *The Cornered Cat:
A Woman's Guide to Concealed Carry*
www.corneredcat.com

PREFACE

My entry into shooting was not a fun one; it began when I received a threat from an ex-boyfriend. I believed he was capable of carrying it out, so I quickly filed a police report. That was when I learned that the police are primarily reactive, that is their role. There is not much they can do to prevent something bad happening unless they happen to be there at the right time. He threatened my life, but since it was verbal and I was not injured, he spent less time at the police station being processed than I did in my first gun class. The situation was an all too common "catch and release" scenario. Please understand, I have a lot of admiration for police officers; they risk their lives for little pay and less respect, but they can't be everywhere at once. A dear friend suggested I get a gun. I had never considered such a thing. In twenty years of military service, I had fired an M-16 once, to qualify before an assignment to South Korea. It did not take me long to see the logic; I took a class, filed for a Concealed Carry Permit, and went shopping. I bought a Ruger P-95, 9mm semi-auto that I still have today. It turned out to be the first of many. Oddly enough, in threatening me, this man opened up a whole new world to me, the world of shooting. Nothing relaxes me like going to the range. I can be cranky, frustrated, angry, but I always walk out with a casual smile, feeling relaxed and contented. Ok, sometimes I shoot particularly well and walk out a little pumped.

I shot casually for years, keeping my permit current, just in case I decided I wanted to carry again. I had a gun at home for emergencies, but unless it was with me, it was useless. The world is a different place than when I was a kid. Today, we wouldn't dream of leaving our doors unlocked and ground level windows open. People do not seem to have the same respect for other people: gangs, flash mobs, muggings. So I started to carry my gun regularly and decided I should practice more regularly. I was reminded how much fun it is to shoot, and I enjoyed seeing my skills improve. I started to wonder how I could share some of this with others and decided to look into teaching. At first I was not sure, but I took the plunge, was certified, and joined a great group of instructors and, for me, the rest is history.

One stupid act of intimidation changed my life in ways he never intended. I found shooting, and the joy I get from it. I found a second family in this wonderful community of shooters. I found a passion for teaching and sharing my joy. I found my voice, authoring a blog and a Facebook page with shooting tips and ideas and occasional humor. I cofounded an event and a nonprofit corporation dedicated to teaching gun safety and encouraging parents to teach their kids, especially their daughters, to shoot, for fun, for self-esteem, for the opportunities it can provide, and for a chance to do things as a family. Moreover, I got the chance to share all of this with a completely new audience, you!

However you came to shooting, welcome! I hope you find the pleasure and joy in it that I do.

Safe Shooting!

Lynne Finch

ACKNOWLEDGMENTS —

So many people deserve my sincere appreciation for bringing me to this point in my life. First, Evan Carson, President of Innovative Defensive Solutions, LLC, who convinced me that I should take the National Rifle Association Pistol Instructor course and then come team with him and his cadre of amazing adjunct instructors. Evan is also my instructor and I have learned more from him than I think even he realizes. Evan helped me discover a passion for teaching and sharing information, and to find my "voice" for writing.

My students, I've learned as much, if not more, from you than you did from me. Your excitement, your questions, your patience, and your smiles all gave me a reason to keep teaching.

Some dear friends who've been incredibly supportive and patient, letting me bounce ideas for feedback and supporting me through this process—Thank you Cathi, Becky Lou, Crystal, Shelby, Nichole, Tom, Doug, William, Dave and Julie.

Thank you to Terri Matthews, who helped me find the courage to take my first shot.

Thank you to Skyhorse Publishing for giving me this chance to share what I've learned, and to Kristin for her careful and patient editorial assistance and handholding of a nervous new author.

Most of all, thank you to my husband, Dr. Russ Charlesworth Jr. Without his patience, understanding, and support, none of this would have been possible. He put up with my constant discussion and long hours of teaching and writing. His love and support and affection, and that of our two precious shelter cats, Rhiannon and Cinnia, helped me keep going when I was tired or frustrated.

I also would like to thank Don McNeil for helping with many of the photographs. He made a very scary aggressor.

Principal photographers for this work were Dr. Russ Charlesworth Jr. and myself.

Chapter 1

WELCOME TO THE WORLD OF SHOOTING

Shooters are a fun-loving, open, and welcoming group, so jump in and share the joy!

Many paths could have led you here. You may have grown up shooting with your dad, you may have a significant other or friends who shoot, or you may be responding to a sense of discomfort and want to know how to protect yourself and your family, or maybe you are just curious. Whatever has led you to pick up this book to learn more, I am glad you are here. One thing to remember: *Shooting is fun*! I carry a tote bag with the following saying on it:

A Bad Day at the Range Beats a Good Day at the Office

I've never met a shooter who would argue with that statement! Have patience and you will discover the joys of this new world.

For me, nothing beats going to the range (when I am stressed, cranky, or just need to relax) and making holes in paper. Truly, it's even better than shopping! (Don't tell my husband!) Not long ago I was feeling very stressed; we had just founded National Take Your Daughter to the Range Day (more on that later) and I was feeling overwhelmed trying to keep up with everything. A sweet lady, and supporter, reminded me that I needed to relax, to just go shoot. In those few words, she reminded me why I do what I do. Years ago (more than I care to admit) I took flying lessons, even soloed a few times, but got to a point where it was too expensive to keep going and gave it up. Learning to fly can be pretty intense. My instructor, who had been a pilot for over forty years, once told me "sometimes you just have to punch holes in clouds." That was his way of telling me I needed to relax and just go, have fun, fly for the sheer joy of being up in the air. Shooting is much the same; it can be intense, scary, noisy, but there is the sheer joy and fun. Reading this book is a first step into the world of shooting, and I hope I can help you to discover that joy for yourself.

Numbers do not lie; more and more women are buying guns and learning to shoot! Gun and ammunition sales are skyrocketing. Shooting used to be a male dominated sport, but there have been stand-out women for hundreds of years. In the 1500s, the earliest settlers had to shoot to eat and defend their homes. The Ladies were a big part of that. Think of Annie Oakley doing trick shots in Buffalo Bill's Wild West Show starting in 1885, and starring for seventeen years. Julie Golob, captain of the Smith & Wesson Professional Shooting Team and author of *Shoot* has been shooting, competing, and winning for more than twenty years! Many young women are standouts from the crowd shooters. A nine-year-old girl, Emily, set the club

MISS ANNIE OAKLEY,
(LITTLE SURE SHOT.)
BUFFALO BILL'S WILD WEST.

Figure 1-1. Annie Oakley

record at a West Texas shooting club with a perfect score shooting Rimfire Silhouettes. She broke the previous record that *she* had set the year before. This was not a record for Juniors, this was *everyone*! I'm not giving out her full information because of her age, but *wow,* she is to be congratulated! I will be watching for her to be one of the next in a long line of successful women shooters!

More and more women are learning to shoot, in classes around the country, some mixed gender, some women-only. They are discovering not only the relaxation that comes with the focus of a trip to the range, but a sense of strength and empowerment that comes from mastering a new skill and knowing you can defend yourself and your family. There can be a sense of camaraderie going to the range with friends. There is a calming focus in going to the range alone.

Statistics are funny things; you can usually manipulate them to depict whatever you want them to. One thing I know is I am seeing more women at the range and in training classes. It appears that more and more women are discovering the joys of shooting. Popular press tells us that more women are joining the shooting community, as are more families. What would be better than a couple of hours at the range with your family? Maybe a couple of hours at the range with your girlfriends? The shooting community is like a big, reasonably functional family. Someone is always ready with advice, assistance, and friendship, to let you try out his or her gun or just point you in the right direction.

Women-only classes are popping up around the country and women's shooting groups are getting easier to find. The National Rifle Association (NRA) has a Women on Target program that promotes this. For some women, they may be more comfortable with other women. Some do not care. If you have been threatened or violated by a man, you might find comfort with a women-only program. I have never participated in a women-only shooting event, although it is on my goal list. I did sing with a Sweet Adeline's Chorus for several years. If someone had told me you could put 100+ women together every week for several hours, keep them focused, even under pressure of competitions and shows and still have a supportive environment, I would not have believed it before that. Now, I know better. I do a lot of research into women's issues with shooting: concealed carry, dressing to hide the gun, shopping for a gun, and more. I have read many books, blogs, talked to and corresponded with many prominent women shooters and authors. Here I have been given the opportunity to share what I have learned with you, all in one place! How much easier could it be? It is up to you if you want to dip your toes in with other women or jump in with a mixed gender group.

I enjoy teaching mixed gender classes. I think it is good for men to see women learning and succeeding right next to them. Guys, be warned, the ladies tend to outshoot you in the beginning classes. It can be good for women, too, to see that they can keep up with, and often exceed, the skills of the men. About twelve years ago, I went shooting with someone I was dating at the time. He had a macho attitude and was (no pun intended) cocky. So, I shot well, but not great, deliberately hitting various areas on the target. We were down to the last magazine of ammo we had brought and he made some stupid comment about how I could get better if I practiced. That did it; I drilled my next ten rounds through the middle of the bull's-eye, laid the gun down, turned around, and just smiled. We did not date much after that. Luckily, my husband, who I met not long after that, was not a serious shooter (he's more of a plinker, can shoot reasonably well, but isn't really interested in it as a sport) but is very supportive. His favorite expression is "If you can't be a gun nut, be a gun nut supporter!" Women should never feel that they need to do less than their best to protect the egos of men, and men should never expect it.

What do you need to get started? Interest and an open mind! Be curious, be interested, and be open to the possibilities. Who knows where they may lead. There are so many possibilities once you start shooting. You can shoot just for fun, or you can practice and try competing. Check out Julie Golob's book *Shoot* for lots of great information on the different types of competition. You can dress up in old west style and join in Cowboy Action shooting, sometimes called Single Action Shooting Society (SASS), where you adopt a name and a persona and dress up like your character and compete, or just go have fun! Women of all ages participate in shooting; from six-year-old girls to ninety-year-old women! This is a sport that transcends gender, age, and many physical limitations. Blind people shoot with a spotter, and I've seen photos of amputees shooting quite well with their feet.

Odds are you know someone who shoots, but do not realize it. Many shooters do not talk about it much because there are people out there who are uncomfortable with the idea of a gun. These people generally fall into one of two categories. There are those with a healthy respect and a little fear but are willing to allow that some people enjoy it. While the other side falls into what we call the "Anti's" category. The Anti's have an irrational hatred for firearms and do not think anyone should have them. My words may be strong, but I believe that we have the right to make decisions for ourselves, but not for other people. A gun is a tool, like a hammer, or a kitchen knife. Well, maybe more complex than a hammer since it has moving parts, but it is still a tool. As such, it deserves respect, and care, but not fear. Are you afraid of your car? That has many more moving parts than a gun, and when used properly and maintained according to the manufacturer's specifications, it is perfectly safe. Same thing can be said about a gun. When used properly, and well maintained, it is perfectly safe. You will notice that I never refer to a gun as a weapon. To me, a weapon is an *offensive* tool; it can be a knife, a bat, a garden implement, or yes, even a gun. A firearm is a *defensive* tool; I will use it for my defense, or my family's, but I will never use it to initiate a confrontation.

Ready for the journey to begin? It's easy! Keep reading and we will have fun together.

Figure 1-2. Ruger LCP with LaserMax

Chapter 2

FINDING AN INSTRUCTOR

You have taken the first step; you have made the decision to try shooting! Great! Now what? There are several options, but I strongly encourage you to start with formal training. You will learn safe gun handling, the fundamentals of shooting, how to stand, how to hold a pistol, how to use your sights, yes, there are two—all before you develop any bad habits that can be tough to unlearn. One school of thought is that it takes 1,000 repetitions to create a habit. In addition, it takes 2,000 to break a habit, then another 1,000 to cement the change. It is so much easier to learn the correct technique in the beginning.

Some people think having their spouse, or significant other, teaching them to shoot would be fine. It might, but ask yourself: would you want your husband to teach you to drive? Also, unless your spouse is a certified instructor, is he, or she, doing everything correctly?

Anyone can call himself or herself a Firearms Instructor. That does not mean all instructors are created equal. I encourage you to look for an NRA Certified Pistol Instructor who is teaching an NRA course, such as First Steps Pistol or Basic Pistol. You could also attend a class at a well-established training institute such as Front Sight in Nevada. The goal is to have a well-trained, and vetted, instructor who is following a tried and tested curriculum. This is especially important in the beginning when you might be a little nervous. Nervous is natural, it is ok. Most of my students are skittish before they fire their first shot, a little calmer after the first shot, and grinning from ear to ear by the fourth or fifth shot!

Figure 2-1. Students Taking Notes in a Class

You can find an NRA certified instructor in your area by visiting the NRA Instructor portal at www.nrainstructors.org, selecting the course(s) you want, inputting your zip code and radius you are willing to travel, and you will see a list of offerings in your area with dates, locations, and contact information. You can also visit your local range or gun store and look for fliers or business cards. You can ask around, odds are you already know someone who shoots; you just might not know it. These people might be able to recommend a good instructor.

I encourage new shooters to start with an NRA First Steps Pistol or Basic Pistol class, or a similar introductory level class. Your course should cover a general introduction to pistols, what the main components are, generally how they work, the basics of cleaning, shooting fundamentals, and some hands-on live fire at a range with an instructor to help you get started.

As more women come to shooting, there are many women-only classes that have begun popping up across the country. So it is up to you if you would prefer a single or mixed gender class. There are also a lot of women's shooting groups; this can be a great source of support and encouragement.

Once you have identified a couple classes or instructors that look interesting, you need to narrow them down to find "the one." But how? Talk to the instructor. If they are *not* willing to spend a few minutes answering questions, move on to the next instructor on your list. If you have to leave a message, or send an email, give them at least twenty-four hours to get back to you. Most of us have day jobs, and we teach shooting because it is our passion. We love it! But that means it can take us a day to get back to you. Once you get in contact, what kinds of questions should you ask? Following are some suggestions that should help you get a sense of the instructor and their personality so you can judge if you would be comfortable with them.

- Are you an NRA Certified Pistol Instructor?
- Are you following an NRA approved curriculum?
- How many students are in an average class?
- Is there range time included in this class?
- What is the ratio of instructors to students on the range? (If it is less than one instructor for every two or three students, consider going to the next instructor on your list.)
- Do I have to have my own pistol or will you have guns I can shoot?
- Are you the one who will be teaching my class, and if not, what can you tell me about the instructor I will have?

- How long have you been teaching?
- What kind of shooting do you do? (The answer you are looking for here can vary depending on the type of shooting you want to do. If you are learning for defense, you want someone who practices defensive shooting techniques. If you are interested in competing, you might want someone who competes.)
- What is the number one priority for this class? (*Safety*!)
- Where will the class be held?
- What range do you use?
- Does the range have eye and ear protection I can borrow?
- Are there any additional costs above the tuition? (This may include having to provide your own ammunition or targets, or pay a range fee.)
- If you have any physical limitations or restrictions you may ask if they have experience with your particular needs.

These should give you a sense of the instructor, and how you will respond to him or her. Ask any other questions you may have, such as "How do you handle nervous students?" Are you comfortable with the person you spoke with, their answers, and attitude? The introduction to shooting can be a little scary and you want someone who you feel comfortable with and trust to lead you through the first shots. If you are not satisfied, keep looking! I promise there is an instructor out there for you. The adage "You have to kiss a lot of toads to find a Prince" applies to finding the perfect instructor. We all have different needs, and there is at least one perfect toad, or instructor, out there for you. Your first class can set the tone for the rest of your shooting experience. If you leave with a huge grin thinking, *That was awesome!* your instructor's job was done well and you will want to come back and do it again! If not, returning to the range can be a little intimidating and might not be a high priority. I have worked with many students on the range, some had shot before, some were afraid to pick up the pistol the first time, and some were so anxious to shoot they were jumpy. One hundred percent of them shared one thing: they left with huge smiles, clutching their targets with nice tight groupings, and were eager to go again!

One great thing about joining a class is the social opportunity it provides. I have seen many students exchanging email addresses and phone numbers after class; they were making new shooting buddies! It can be fun and encouraging having someone to shoot with. You might have an off day, but shooting buddies can support you. Next time it might be them having an off day. We all go through it. I have gone to the range and shot horrible! I have to slow myself down, remind myself that I know what I am doing, mentally review the basics, and start over. It is a lot like doing a reboot of my computer. Then, I shoot more like my expectations for myself. We all go through it, if you have an off day, just reboot, go back to the basics, and start fresh.

Figure 2-2. Instructor and Student on the Range

When I decided to become an instructor, I looked on the NRA website to find a certification class. I found several in my area and left phone messages. Evan Carson, president of Innovative Defensive Solutions, LLC, my instructor, was the first one to call me back.

We talked, I expressed some hesitation when he told me about what I would need to do to qualify (shoot at 50 feet, handle a revolver, etc.). I started thinking maybe I needed more training. He gently convinced me to meet him at the range and shoot and he would give me his feedback on if he thought I was ready. That was when I knew this was someone I wanted to learn from. He showed me a couple things that made a huge difference in my grouping and in ten minutes took me from a six-inch group to a two-inch group. Ok, now I was excited and wanted more. Not only did I take the pistol instructor class, I went on to become an Adjunct Instructor (a type of subcontractor) for him and started sitting in on classes and very soon teaching them. I've also picked up some additional certifications along the way.

I've had excited students, nervous students, young, old, steady, shaky, but I've never had a student leave without a huge smile. It is ok to be nervous, or excited. This is something new, something unknown, and maybe even a little scary. I've always heard that jumping out of a plane the first time was easy, it was the second jump that was tough. This is not so for shooting. The first shot might be a little scary, you don't really know what to expect, you are trusting your instructor to help you and they will. The second shot is easier, and it just keeps getting better.

Chapter 3

YOUR FIRST TRIP TO THE RANGE

You found an instructor, you have taken your first class, and now you are ready for your first trip to the range. Congratulations on making it to this point! What do you need to know? Not all ranges are created equal. Some are simple outdoor setups and some are state of the art indoor establishments with electronic target carriers, good lighting, and more. Most fall somewhere in between.

Each range has its own set of rules and it is your responsibility to learn and follow them. If there is anything you do not understand, ask your instructor or a Range Safety Officer (RSO); they are generally easy to spot, often in a red or fluorescent shirt, some insignia where you can spot it easily. Outdoor ranges are generally not as loud as indoor ranges but you also have weather, sun, insects, and occasionally some interesting facilities—the third tree to the left is Men, the fifth bush on the right is Women, although most have at least rudimentary restrooms. The choice is yours, go where you are comfortable, where you feel welcome, and where you feel safe.

Dressing to Shoot

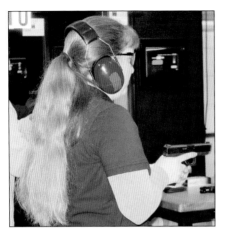

Figure 3-1. Student in Proper Attire and Safety Equipment

When you take your first adventure to the shooting range it's important to carefully consider your outfit. Do you need special clothes? No, but you do need practical clothes. There are some basic safety considerations when you are dressing to go shoot. Besides your safety gear (eye and ear protection) you should wear something with a high neckline (no flashing cleavage at the range, I will explain why a little later) like a t-shirt or a button-up top. Closed-toe shoes are also important, preferably flat, or nearly so, especially when you are starting out. I wear high heels to work but not to shoot. They affect my balance and my center of gravity and I want to keep a stable stance when I am shooting. Outdoor ranges can be a lot of fun, fresh air, interesting choice of targets; depending on the range you may shoot paper, steel, reactive steel, old cars, or bowling pins! Remember to dress for the weather by bringing sunscreen, bug spray, bottled water, and tinted shooting glasses. A baseball cap can help to deflect brass away from your face.

Brass? If you are shooting a semi-automatic pistol or a rifle, the cartridge case, which holds the primer, powder and bullet (the bullet is just one component of the cartridge, it is the projectile that is pushed out of the gun by pressure from the burning powder) is ejected from the pistol as the gun cycles between shots. This cartridge case is commonly referred to as "brass" regardless of what it is made out of: brass, steel, aluminum. Brass has three primary characteristics. First, as it is ejected, it is *hot*! Second, it is unpredictable, it can go almost any direction, and you do not know which direction it will fly or where it will end up. Third, it seems to be attracted to places it should not be, such as between your toes if you are wearing sandals, in your glasses, but especially down your cleavage—you just never know. Ninety-nine out of one hundred times it will land harmlessly on the floor or ground, but when they do not ...

The Brass Dance

The Brass Dance is what happens when a piece of hot brass lands where it should not. It is not frequent, but if you keep shooting, it will happen. You will always remember your first time! When it finds you, it is *critical* to stay safe. Calmly take your finger off the trigger, lay your pistol on the shooting table pointed down range, step back from the booth or firing line and *get it out*! This is the Brass Dance. Somewhere between a spastic Chicken Dance and the Hokey Pokey in appearance. Some women have been known to rip their tops off, much to the delight of the men, but you probably will not need to do that. The most efficient method, if you are able, is to grab the brass through your shirt and pull it away from your body. Your hand is protected by the shirt, the brass cools quickly, and once you pull it away, as long as you are not tucked in, you can let it drop harmlessly to the floor. A good reason not to tuck in your top! Don't be surprised if you find a stray cartridge when you get home. I have had them in my slacks, in my bra, I've even had it go down inside a snug turtleneck! Sometimes I don't realize it and then when I get home and go to change clothes, brass will fall out onto the floor. I've been shooting with someone and had them flick brass off my shoulder (which can be a little disconcerting, having someone reach over unexpectedly, but he was trying to be helpful).

You will see some smiles, maybe a couple of chuckles, but most of us have been there and the support is good-natured. Think of this—there are two types of shooters, those who *have* done the Brass Dance and those who *will* do the Brass Dance.

Eye and Ear Protection

Often referred to simply as Eyes and Ears, they are very important. You want to ensure that you are using glasses that are designed, and rated, for shooting sports. They come in a variety of designs, colors, and lens tints but they should be marked as complying with ANSI standards Z87.1 and/or Z87.3, which refers to minimum impact resistance. If you wear prescription lenses, you will probably notice some people on the range wearing their prescription glasses. However, your glasses are expensive, probably not rated for the same level of impact resistance and can chip if hit by a piece of brass. Then you have an annoying spot on your lens that won't go away. You can find shooting glasses designed to fit over your regular glasses for twenty dollars or less. Much less expensive than replacing your glasses, or worse, having shards removed from your eye. I do not recommend purchasing special prescription shooting glasses unless you become a serious competitor. They are expensive, and later, if you find yourself in a self-defense situation you may not have those glasses. It is better to practice with what you live your life in.

Hearing protection, or "ears," are also critical. Some guns, like a .22 caliber, make very little noise. Some sound like cannons going off. Most are somewhere in between. You may find an outdoor range that does not require hearing protection, but use it anyway! Your hearing can be damaged by exposure to loud noises and once gone, you might never get it back. Quality ears are often available to borrow from the range. The more you shoot, the more likely you will want to buy your own. Check the ratings for decibel level and buy the highest rating in your price range. Electronic ears block loud noises but still allow you to speak to your instructor or shooting buddy without yelling. This can be a great asset. If you have sensitive ears, consider inserting little foam earplugs, like you can find in the drugstore to block the sound of a snoring spouse, under your ears for extra protection.

You can even find them in pink at outlets like Amazon or web stores that specialize in women's shooting accessories.

One final consideration, any chance you are pregnant? While most ranges will allow you to shoot, it is usually discouraged, and you may want to wait. This is a decision for you and your doctor, but understand the baby will be exposed to lead and loud noises. It is something to consider, and unless there is a pressing need to practice, it might be best to wait until after the baby is born. In the interim, you should still be able to dry fire to help maintain your skills. Dry fire is explained in greater detail later in Chapter 9, Practice, Practice, Practice. If you have a Concealed Carry Permit, you can still carry for your own defense; just be mindful that your center of gravity shifts as your belly grows and you can be off balance. Check out concealed carry tips in Chapter 18, Holsters and Dressing to Carry Concealed.

Figure 3-2. Eyes and Ears

Chapter 4

CYLINDERS, SLIDES AND ACTIONS...OH MY!

A *revolver* is a pistol with a rotating cylinder that holds the ammunition and rotates when the hammer is cocked to align the next chamber with the firing pin.

A *semi-automatic*, often called a semi-auto, has a magazine that holds the cartridges and serves as the source of ammunition. The action of the slide being propelled back by the gasses and force released from the burning powder, which also propels the bullet forward out of the casing and down the barrel, causes the spent (or used) casing to be ejected and a fresh round to be pushed into place by the spring and carrier plate of the magazine.

Both revolvers and semi-autos can have an external hammer or an internal mechanism (a hammer or striker) which is activated when the trigger is pulled.

Basic actions are common between revolvers and semi-autos.

- Single Action (SA), the trigger performs one function: it releases the hammer, which must be cocked manually.
- Double Action (DA), the trigger cocks and releases the hammer, or resets the striker.

- Single/Double Action (SA/DA) is a semi-auto where the first shot is double action and the subsequent shots are single action. The action of the slide being pushed back cocks the hammer or resets the striker and prepares the gun to fire the next round in single action.

Double Action is usually a longer, harder trigger pull. Most double action pistols have the option of manually cocking the hammer (provided there is one) so the gun may also be fired in Single Action mode. Not all guns with an external hammer can be manually cocked, so please check your owner's manual to be sure!

So, revolver or semi-auto? External hammer or not? These are personal preferences and are dependent on how you plan to use your pistol. Revolvers have fewer moving parts, but hold significantly fewer rounds and generally tend to have harder trigger pulls. Semi-autos have more parts to deal with but can hold a lot more rounds, depending on the model. Hammers may catch on clothing if carrying it concealed, but hammerless or shrouded hammers cannot be manually cocked and shot in SA.

The key is to find a gun that fits your hand, your shooting style, and that is comfortable enough to practice with.

Figure 4-1. This Smith & Wesson Bodyguard 38 is an example of a Double Action Revolver.

Chapter 5

NAME THAT PART!

The following illustrations are intended to help you identify parts of the gun to aid with terminology and familiarity. Knowing the basic components of your firearm and how they work helps you gain confidence as well as lets you ask questions. It's important to understand how they fit together and operate, in case there is ever a malfunction that you need to fix in a hurry.

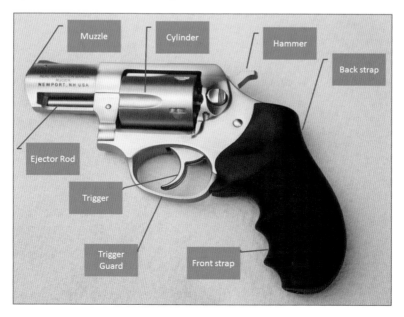

Figure 5-1. Ruger SP101 - Revolver

Figure 5-2. Glock 19 - 9mm Semi-Automatic

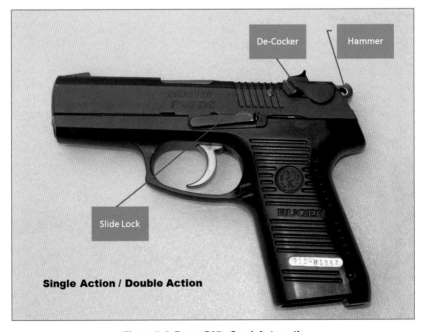

Figure 5-3. Ruger P95 - Semi-Automatic

Chapter 6

BUYING YOUR FIRST GUN

When shopping for a gun, you need to use the Goldilocks approach. This one is too big, this one is too small … until … ahh, this one is *just right*! If you have friends who shoot, ask if you can try out their guns to get a feel for different types and calibers. If you take a basic pistol class, be sure there is range time included and that guns are made available for your use if you do not have one. This is a great opportunity to learn more about guns, safe gun handling, and some of the "gun-speak" so when you go shopping you can ask for what you want to see. What is just right for me may not be just right for you. We have different-sized hands and different hand and arm strength. Do you want something for home defense or to go "play" at the range? You may prefer something you can carry comfortably.

Be leery of the cute little "pocket pistols," such as the Kel-Tec, Ruger LCP, or the Smith & Wesson Feather Weight. They are easy to conceal but deceptively difficult to shoot without a lot of practice. They can also be tough on the wrist. Similarly, a .44 magnum may seem like a cannon in the female hand, even many men have difficulty shooting them. Watch out for the recoil. Some men enjoy putting something like that in a woman's hands and assuring her "it doesn't have much recoil." Well, they lie. These jokers think they are funny, I think of them as ex-friends.

Figure 6-1. Kel-Tec P-3AT

When I bought my first gun, I was in a little bit of a hurry. I believed I needed to be able to defend myself right away. I went into a gun store and threw myself on the mercy of the man behind the counter. I got lucky. They were compassionate and knowledge-able. I walked out with a Ruger P95 (9mm semi-auto) and promptly went to a nearby range and practiced for a couple hours until my arms ached, my thumb bled from loading magazines (I had a lot to learn about how to do that without wearing a hole in my thumb) and my targets had nice, big, satisfying holes in them. I felt like I could hit what I was aiming at and thought that was good enough. It was only after I started taking more formal training that I realized I had a lot of habits to unlearn and new techniques to use to make my shooting more accurate.

Many gun shop employees will point women to a revolver, citing the simple operation and that you do not need to rack the slide. This is true; however, while their function may be more simple, they can be harder to shoot than a semi-automatic, with barely-there sights and a heavy trigger pull. If you think a revolver is the way you want to go, ask your instructor if he or she has one you can try before you buy. With Charter Arms' introduction of revolvers in colors, such as pink, turquoise, lavender, and even leopard, they have become more popular. I do kind of like the idea of matching my gun to my shoes, and occasionally enjoy shooting a revolver. However, I personally prefer a semi-automatic as my primary firearm. This is just my preference. Some people would never carry anything but a revolver. It comes down to what you are most comfortable with.

Figure 6-2. Charter Arms Pink Lady Off-Duty

It is amazing to me how often I've had someone (usually a man) try to tell me that a little gun, like the Ruger LCP or the Smith & Wesson Feather Weight revolver, is a great carry gun for a woman. They say things like "it isn't a good range gun, you wouldn't want to shoot it for fun, but in a dangerous situation your adrenaline will be up and you will hardly feel the recoil." Really? Ok, think about what happens when you put a lot of power, like a .38+P, through a gun that weighs 15 ounces, or a .380 round through something that weighs 9.4 ounces? You are going to have control issues. Can you overcome that? Sure. *With practice.* This means taking it to the range and shooting it—a lot! I like little guns, they are cute, easy to conceal, and handy; I own a Ruger LCP for that reason. The first time I took it to the range, I seriously questioned my judgment in buying it. However, I stuck it out, practiced, and got proficient. I also got a very sore wrist. My instructor (who has six inches and seventy pounds on me) shot it and while he had fewer control issues, he really didn't like it. Will I ever get to the point where I think it is fun to shoot? Probably not. Will I trust it as a backup gun? *Yes!* Will I carry it as a primary? No, I have had too many malfunctions with it. For me it is a last resort gun. I do have a Ruger LC9, which is only slightly larger, less than an inch in length longer, but nearly twice the weight. It shoots 9mm, that I have no problems with at all. It has become my favorite backup gun. Will I carry it alone? Only in very rare circumstances where I really cannot conceal my Glock 19 on my body because I am in a dress, evening wear or something special. Why? My Glock magazine holds 15 rounds, and my LC9 magazine holds 7. The odds of needing 15 are slim, but I sure would like to have them if I need them!

For the average woman, a 9mm semi-automatic is a good place to start. The tiny guns are popular, but they are not kind to begin-ners. You are putting a lot of power through something that weighs less than your shoe. Once you are more experienced, they can be handy, easy to carry and conceal, but they are not fun for practice. Small is not easy to control; however, just because a gun is larger does not mean it will not fit in your hand. Fit is key.

One concern many women have is racking the slide on a semi-automatic—this is the act of pulling the slide as far as it will go and letting it go home using the power of the internal spring to chamber a round. I always tell my students to "pull it all the way back and let it fly." You can cause a malfunction if you ride it forward (do not let go but keep your hand on the slide as it returns forward). You *can* rack the slide, with practice.

How many times have you heard that women do not have the hand strength to rack the slide on a semi-automatic? Some men out there have trouble with it! If you are a new shooter and find racking the slide a challenge, that is ok. Do not give up! You can do a couple things. It really is more about technique and leverage than it is about strength.

First, position is key. Have a firm grip on the pistol with your strong hand (the one you write with). This should be similar to your shooting grip. You can pull the gun in close to your body, which gives you better leverage. With the nondominant hand or your support hand, cup the top rear of the slide (it is often ridged to make it easier to grasp), being careful to ensure that your hand does not extend over the ejection port (this is important as you do not want a round to go up into your hand or get stuck because your hand is blocking it), and pull straight back while pushing forward with your strong hand. Pull the slide all the way straight to the rear, and then let it go. Yes, let it fly, if you hold the slide as it is returning to position you can create several issues such as a misfeed or failure of the gun to go into battery (be ready to fire). This takes practice. It is also harder on a tiny gun; you may need to adjust the position, but you can do it! You do not want to "slingshot" the slide, which is grasping from the rear and pulling back, then letting go. This involves fine motor skills, versus gross motor skills that we use in the overhand method. When you are stressed, or panicked, fine motor skills can desert you faster than cheap friends when the dinner check arrives.

The ejection port is where the brass is ejected. You do not want to develop a habit of covering it when you rack the slide. There may be times when you need to rack the slide as part of clearing a malfunction. You do not want your hand to block a cartridge from being ejected, released, or worse!

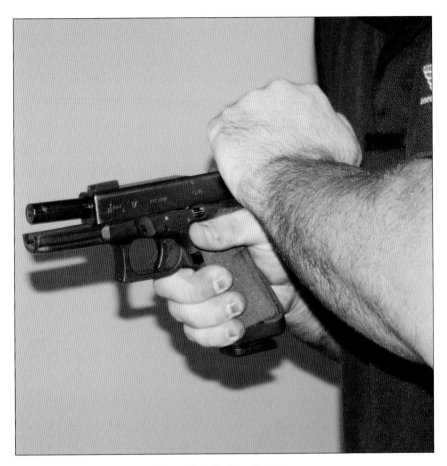

Figure 6-3. Racking the Slide

If you need to strengthen your hands, there are products available for that purpose. My personal favorite is the Grip Master, available in multiple resistance levels. It may be used to work the fingers individually. The other advantage to this exercise is that it helps with your trigger control. Some triggers are harder to pull than others. Ironically, the triggers on revolvers, which do not have a slide and are often recommended to women, usually have a harder trigger pull (more pounds of pressure) than most semi-automatics.

Lastly, a good instructor can help you to adjust your hand positions so that you can be more effective. Do not hesitate to ask for help. If

Figure 6-4. Grip Master

you are at a range that has NRA certified range safety officers, they are usually instructor certified, or at the very least experienced shooters, and therefore can offer you some advice or assistance if you need it.

Once you have chosen a revolver or semi-automatic, you must consider caliber. For a new shooter who is looking to shoot for fun or for self-defense, a 9mm semi-automatic or a revolver in .32 or .38 caliber is a great place to start. They are economical to shoot, not overwhelming or overpowering. The number refers to the diameter of the cartridge. Bigger cartridges, or those with Magnum +P or +P+ designations, can be a lot harder to control and may not work in your gun. Check your owner's manual for specifications on the acceptable ammunition. One note: some .38 revolvers will also fire .357 rounds. Smaller number, easier to shoot? No! I have a .38/.357. I fired one .357 round through it. Yep, *one!* It took two weeks for the bruise on my hand to go away; however, I did not hit myself in the head! If in doubt, ask an instructor or knowledgeable shooter.

The most important thing is the fit to *your* hand. Not too big, not too small, but Just Right! You need to pick up the gun, hold it in your shooting grip. Does your finger easily reach the trigger? Can you wrap both hands around the grip comfortably? Can you reach the magazine release or the hammer spur without breaking your shooting grip? If not, and you do not have unusually small hands, keep shopping. Manufacturers know that more and more women are buying firearms and they are making them in configurations that are more comfortable to the female hand. The key area of fit is the back strap to the trigger. Can you comfortably hold the gun and reach the trigger? This is more important than the "size" or caliber of the gun. If you cannot hold it, you cannot control it!

Figure 6-5. Strong Hand, Back Strap to Trigger

Bottom line is fit the gun to you. For average-sized people, it should be fairly easy to find something comfortable. If you have unusually small, or large, hands, you can have a gunsmith alter your pistol to fit you better. Some models have an adjustable back strap; Smith & Wesson makes some that you can adapt quite easily. Women do not need tiny pocket guns, and men do not need hand cannons. Neither is easy to control. As you become more experienced, have fun experimenting with small and large guns, but when you are starting out you need something that you are comfortable with, that does not hurt your hand, and that you will use to practice!

I encourage you to buy your gun from an established dealer. There are some great deals, and more to choose from than in the average store, to be found at gun shows, but make sure that you can find the dealer again if you have questions or a problem. New or used is up to you and your budget, but if buying used, it is especially important that you have some type of warranty from the dealer. You can expect to pay from $300 to $500 and up for a pistol, depending on the manufacturer and features. When you are buying your gun, factor in the price of the ammunition you will need to practice. Some guns are fussy and prefer specific brands. Some, like the Glock, will shoot almost anything. The caliber has a big impact on the price. A box of .22 cartridges can be very inexpensive, a box of .44 magnums can be quiet expensive, with 9mm and .38 somewhere in the middle.

Another consideration, after revolver or semi-automatic, is what type of shooting you will do. This is an investment so think long term, next month, next year. Do you see yourself going to the range for socialization and plinking? Do you see yourself using your firearm for home defense? Do you plan to get a concealed carry permit? A gun that is good for carry and home defense can also be a great range gun, but a plinking gun may not be the best choice for carry or home defense. As an example, my Browning Buckmark .22 is great fun at the range and inexpensive to shoot, but I could not begin to carry it.

Can you get more than one? Sure, and most of us do end up with more than one, but starting out, it is wise to consider your budget and maximize the utility of your investment.

Figure 6-6. Browning Buckmark - .22 Target Pistol with Non-stock Accessories

Manual Safety or Not?

This is a matter of preference. My carry guns do not have a manual safety, or if they do, I don't use them. It is one more thing to defeat if I need it. My best safety is my brain. If I stay smart, sane and safe, I don't believe I need a little button. Remember, a manual safety is a mechanical device that can break or fail, so stay smart.

Gun Store Etiquette

Ladies, there is a good chance that you will find a man behind the counter at the gun store. Do not be surprised if you are addressed as "Little Lady." Things are changing but it still happens. They are not being rude, it is a different mindset. If you go to the store with a man, odds are very high that the clerk will address his comments to him, even though you are the one shopping. Politely let him know *you* are the one buying the gun.

I did a little "mystery shopper" exercise where I went into unfamiliar gun stores and pretended to be a newbie. I wanted to see how I would be treated by someone who didn't know me, or know I was an instructor. The older men were quite consistent: revolvers, little guns, and a few pink guns for good measure. One even suggested a two-shot derringer. If you don't know, they are about the size of a baby carrot, and about as much fun to hold onto. I don't necessarily think it is a generational difference, although the younger men tended to make fewer assumptions. I think gun store employees need more education about women shooters, what we need, what we want, and how to help us choose the right gun. Some shops were great, but I found that they tended to be staffed by instructors. Eventually I would give myself away, racking a slide or not muzzling (pointing the gun at) the clerk and they would know.

It is ok to pick up the gun to see how it feels—just be sure the clerk shows you that it is clear and unloaded first. There is rarely a safe direction, and it can be very hard not to point it at anyone, but try, and *keep your finger off the trigger* when you pick it up. If you have any questions about how it functions or how hard it is to take apart, ask! If they do not know, they can look at the owner's manual with you. If you want to try racking the slide, or get a feel for the trigger pull, that is usually fine. However, it is polite to ask first. They want to make a sale, they will say yes, but they will respect you for asking and not scaring them.

Once you have found *your* gun, it is a good time to get a basic cleaning kit. There are often starter kits available with everything you need. They are sized by the caliber of your firearm. You can also buy the components separately and we will address cleaning more in a later chapter. For now, focus on buying the basics:

- Bore Cleaner
- Gun Oil (Gun Oil and Bore Cleaner are two separate chemicals, disregard the packages that claim to be both in one)
- Bore Brush sized for your gun
- Jag or Slotted Tip

Figure 6-7. Basic Cleaning Kit

- Cleaning Rod
- Patches sized for your gun
- Cleaning Brush

Do not be nervous, cleaning it is not much harder than doing your nails!

Now that you have brought your new gun home, you are holding it, getting the feel of it, getting comfortable—it is time to name it! Why? Why not? We name all kinds of things, I name my guns. It makes a personal attachment or bond between you and your gun. It also lets you talk in "code" in public with people who might want to talk about your gun, and you can discuss "Sally" instead of "my Smith and Wesson." Great for the security line at the airport where you *do not* want to say the word *gun*. I name all my guns using the first letter of the manufacturer as the first letter of the name. For example, I have Rachael, Rue and Raven Ruger, Glory and Grace Glock, and Glinda the Good Glock. I have a Henry rifle I named Harmony. I let my husband name my Browning. He called it "Bud." He doesn't get to name them anymore. Find what is meaningful to you. I know someone who purchased an antique Russian-made rifle and named it Anastasia. Sometimes you just know, sometimes you have to shoot it a few times. My first Glock earned her name after our first trip to the range; my response after firing a couple magazines was Oh Glory! Hence, Glory became the name.

Figure 6-8. Glock 19 – Glory, Grace, and Glinda the Good Glock

Chapter 7

SHOOTING FUNDAMENTALS

The number one fundamental is *Safety*!

The National Rifle Association (NRA) has three Safety Rules:

1. *Always* keep the gun pointed in a safe direction.
2. *Always* keep your finger off the trigger until you are ready to shoot.
3. *Always* keep the gun unloaded until you are ready to use it.

Note the emphasis on *Always*. These rules are in this order for a reason, and if you follow these rules, you dramatically increase your safety and the safety of those around you. You still need to be careful and smart, but understanding the basic safety rules is the first step.

Shooting Platform

This refers to your stance. When startled we tend to face what startled us, to square off to it. This is a reflex and the "isosceles" position takes advantage of this and is a great start for beginners. Stand comfortably, feet about shoulder width apart, knees relaxed, weight a little forward on the balls of your feet, head erect and bending slightly forward at the waist. This gives you a stable platform to absorb the recoil and to keep your balance. If you lean back, you are not balanced to absorb the recoil and it can interfere with your ability to reacquire your target.

Figure 7-1. Shooting Stance Shown from Above

We all have a dominant eye, just like we have a dominant hand, and it may, or may not, be on the same side. It does not really matter at this point in your shooting life, but it is still good to know. There are several ways to determine your dominant eye. One is to form a small triangle with your hands, extend your arms straight out and focus on a fixed point looking through the triangle with both eyes. Now, slowly bring your hands back toward your face, keeping the fixed point centered in your view. You will come back to your dominant eye.

Another option to determine your dominant eye is to hold up your index finger at arm's length. With both eyes open, align your finger with a fixed point. Close one eye, open it, and close the

Figure 7-2. Shooting Stance Shown from Side

Figure 7-3. Dominant Eye Exercise

other. With one eye, the relative alignment stays about the same, with the other, the object appears to jump away. The dominant eye is the one with the same relative alignment as both eyes. This is important if you tend to squint when you shoot. Understand that if you are attempting to sight with your nondominant eye, you will always miss your target, by a little or a lot depending on the distance.

If your dominant eye and hand are not on the same side this is called cross dominant. It is not uncommon. Some schools would have you think you need to shoot with the opposite hand, but why make it harder on yourself? Especially with the isosceles position, it really will not matter. As you progress, you can learn to shoot with either hand, but in the beginning, shoot with the hand that is most comfortable for you!

Grip

This is very important. If you are not holding the gun correctly, how can you control it? Your grip starts with your strong hand; you lay your hand on the gun in the start of your shooting grip, index finger along the frame, other fingers in the front of the grip, or front strap. The thumb is beginning to wrap around the back strap, and the web between your thumb and index finger is starting to tuck in high on the back strap.

For a semi-automatic, you will pick up the pistol and bring the heel of the support hand in against the heel of your strong hand, fitting them together like puzzle pieces. Wrap your support hand fingers over your strong hand fingers, under the trigger guard and align your thumbs pointing forward, along the frame.

For a revolver, the primary difference is the thumbs. You will cross your thumbs, weak over strong. This keeps them away from the cylinder, where hot gasses are expelled, and frees your weak thumb to cock the hammer without breaking the shooting grip.

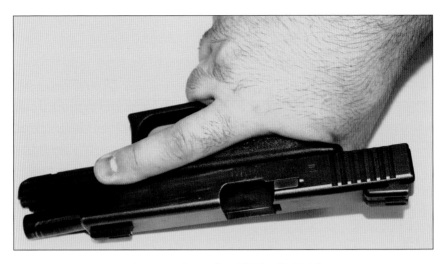

Figure 7-4. Strong Hand Picking Up Pistol

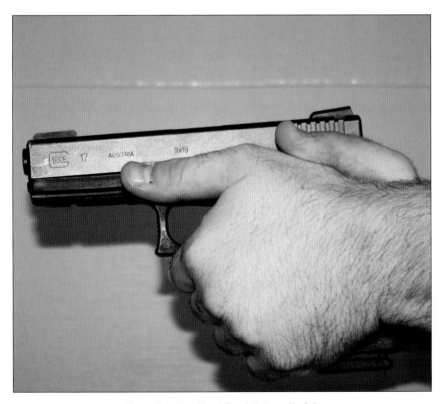

Figure 7-5. Two Hand Semi-Automatic Grip

Figure 7-6. Two Hand Revolver Grip

Loading Your Pistol

To load a semi-automatic, you start by loading the cartridges into your magazine. It has a follow plate and a spring that compresses as you add rounds. You can use your thumb to press down on the back of the rounds as you are pushing them in from the front of the magazine. The magazine will have an open front and then "lips" over approximately 2/3 of the top. The edge of the cartridge case, or rim, will catch under these "lips," this is what keeps the round from popping back out as you load them.

Bring the pistol into your work space, this is about midway between your navel and shoulder, in close to your body. Loading, reloading, and clearing a malfunction should all be done in your work space. It gives you good control, and later, when you are more advanced and practicing for home and/or self-defense you will find

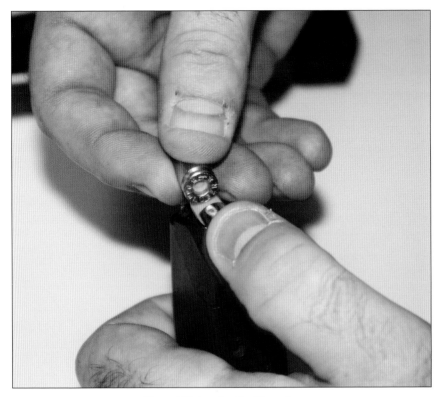

Figure 7-7. Loading the Magazine

that keeping the gun in close to your body minimizes the risk of someone grabbing your gun.

To insert a magazine into the mag well (the opening at the base of the grip), align your index finger along the front of the magazine; this is called "indexing." Then hold the gun in close to your body, angled slightly but pointed in a safe direction, and use your index finger to help guide the magazine into the gun. You also do not need to watch it go in once you have a good feel for it. In an emergency you want to be able to be looking up, seeing all that is around you, not looking down. You do not need to slap it in, just ease it in until you feel it click, then give it a slight tug to ensure it is secure. You can damage the magazine, or the magazine catch, if you slam it in. Now, rack the slide, support hand cupped over the rear of the slide, pistol

Figure 7-8. In your work space

Figure 7-9. Why you operate in your work space

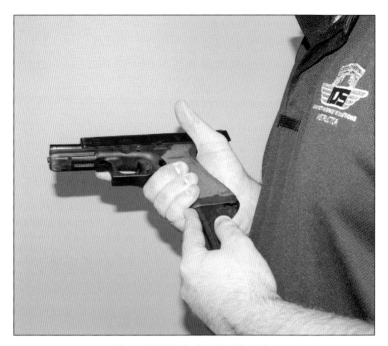

Figure 7-10. Indexing the Magazine

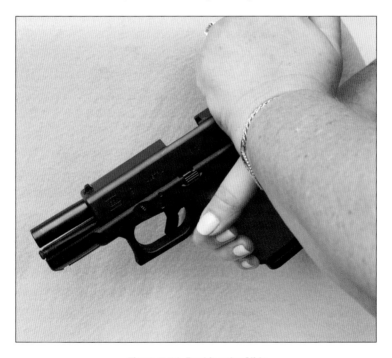

Figure 7-11. Racking the Slide

in close to the body, pull straight back and let go. Sometimes it is easier to use a push/pull motion to rack the slide.

To unload the semi-automatic, you press the magazine release button, letting the magazine fall out. Get into the habit of letting the magazine drop right from the beginning of your training. They aren't fragile and later, when you are working on defensive skills, you will already have the habit of letting it fall as you are reaching for a fresh magazine to reload. Next, rack the slide several times to ensure you have removed any rounds. Then, pull the slide all the way back while pushing up on the slide lock to lock it back, showing clear (unloaded and safe).

Figure 7-12. Clear and Locked Back Semi-Automatic

To load a revolver, open the cylinder using the cylinder release button. Using your support hand, push the cylinder out gently and rest the pistol in your hand with your fingers curled over the cylinder. This frees your strong hand to insert the rounds.

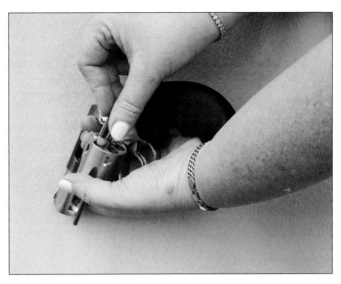

Figure 7-13. Loading a Revolver

To unload the revolver, use the same process as loading to open the cylinder and rest it in your support hand. Then, tilting slightly upward to let gravity help, you can use your thumb, or your strong hand, to press the ejector rod. There is a star plate on the end of the rod that will help to catch and extract any casings, pulling them out of the cylinder.

Figure 7-14. Unloading a Revolver

Sight Picture and Sight Alignment

This is one of the most important fundamentals. Without good sight picture and sight alignment, you will never hit what you are aiming at. You want to align your sights, and yes, there are two! I once had a student who was very surprised, after years of shooting, to learn that. The rear sight, at the back of the slide or frame, is generally a "V"- or a "U"-shaped notch. The front sight is generally a post. They may or may not have colored markings, dots, or outlines. As you are looking at your sights, they should be aligned on your target. Looking through the rear sight you see the front sight centered and even, and beyond that is your target. My instructor likes to say "Top knife edges equal, equal light on both sides."

If your target is small, such as the hole from the last round, your front sight will cover it and you will not actually see it. So where do you focus? The Front Sight! Your rear sight and target will be slightly blurry and your front sight should be in sharp focus.

Each shot fired will have three sight pictures. One right before you fire, one as you are riding the recoil up and then driving back down, and the third as you reacquire your target and prepare for the next shot. Even if you are not planning to take another shot, you want to complete the follow through of riding the recoil up, driving your sights back down and reacquiring your target, then decide if you are, or are not, taking another shot. It is good to practice for a worst case scenario.

Figure 7-15. Perfect Sight Picture

Sight Picture is what you see when you are looking down the barrel of your gun. Sight Alignment is the relationship of your sights to your target.

Trigger Control

One of the most common mistakes for new shooters is poor trigger control. Using just the front tip of your index finger, between the end and the first joint, ease the trigger straight back to a surprise break,

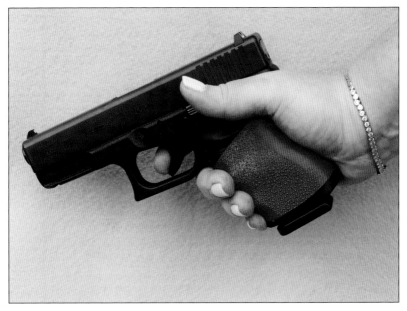

Figure 7-16. Finger on the Trigger

that means you are not anticipating the gun firing. Bang, now hold the trigger back for a fraction of a second and then ease it out until it resets. For most guns there is a "click" you can feel. Some guns have a double click, and a few do not have a perceptible click at all but you will learn how far is far enough for your gun. You do not need to remove your finger from the trigger or to jerk it. Smooth, steady pressure and release to the reset.

Riding the Recoil

It is much easier than riding a mechanical bull (and yes, I have done that once). Recoil is the muzzle rise that occurs as a result of the bullet exiting the barrel. Your goal is to minimize the effect by riding it up and driving it back down as quickly and smoothly as you can and then reacquiring your target. Don't fight it or you are likely to anticipate the recoil, driving the gun down before you actually fire. Let it happen, but control it to minimize the time it takes to reacquire your target.

Most Important Tip!

Relax! This is *fun*! After the first shot, all the rest are easy. Unlike jumping out of a plane where the second time is the hardest, or so I've heard. Like any skill, it takes time to learn, so be patient, have fun, and watch yourself improve!

Chapter 8

MALFUNCTIONS

There are three primary malfunctions that are related to ammunition.

A Misfire is when you pull the trigger and hear *click* instead of *bang*. This may be caused by degraded or damaged ammunition. If you are at a range, keep your pistol pointed down range and slowly count to thirty. This is because you may be experiencing a hang fire.

A *hang fire* is a delay in the ignition of the powder charge. The difference between a misfire and a hang fire is a hang fire eventually goes *bang*, or *pop* possibly several seconds after you have pulled the trigger. When you first hear the click, it is impossible to determine which it is. Be safe and wait 30 seconds before you clear the round.

After 30 seconds, with a revolver, pull the trigger again and the cylinder will rotate to the next round. If you are shooting a semi-automatic, you should release the magazine, and then rack the slide several times to remove the round. If it does not eject, you may need to lock the slide back and tilt the gun, even shake it. As a last resort, you may need to gently pry the round out. If you are uncertain, raise your hand and have a range safety officer assist you. *Always* keep the gun pointed down range the entire time and *never* leave the range with a damaged round still in the chamber. Also, do not attempt to reshoot the round.

The third ammunition-related malfunction is a *squib*. It may sound like sushi, but actually a squib is not found in the ocean, but more likely part way down the barrel of your gun. Signs that a squib round has occurred include: a much quieter or otherwise unusual-sounding discharge noise, lighter than usual or nonexistent recoil force, a discharge of smoke from the ejection port instead of the barrel, and a failure of the action to cycle (in semi-automatic firearms). This can come from poor quality, old or damaged ammunition, or from low quality reloads. When the primer and powder are ignited in the cartridge, a charge is generated that is insufficient to propel the bullet out of the gun. However, this does not mean that no charge is generated, or that it might not have a delayed discharge. If you think you might have a squib, *do not* fire a second round in an attempt to clear the barrel—this can be very dangerous. If you are not familiar with the procedure to clear it, stay in place, keep the gun in your control, pointed down range, and wave for a range safety officer to come and assist you. *Do not* lay the gun down, or remove the gun from the live fire area of the range with the round still in the barrel. In rare cases, this may require the services of a gunsmith but that is still better than a negligent discharge on the way to the car.

How can you minimize your risk of an ammunition-related malfunction? Buy quality ammunition and store it in the original packaging, in a clean, dry environment. If the box appears to have gotten wet or greasy, or the ammunition is old, most ranges have a means to safely dispose of bad ammunition. The price may be tempting, but I do not recommend buying reloads at a gun show. You do not have the same quality control that you get in a factory setting. If you do your own reloads, take your time and focus on the task. Do not try to reload while watching a movie.

If you are in an emergency situation, where you are using your gun to defend yourself, tap the bottom of the magazine to ensure it is seated, rack the slide to eject the damaged round and cycle a fresh one in, and reacquire your target as fast as you can. This drill is called *Tap, Rack, and Reacquire* (it used to be called Tap, Rack, Boom, but you really need to reacquire and reassess your target to make a shoot/no shoot decision).

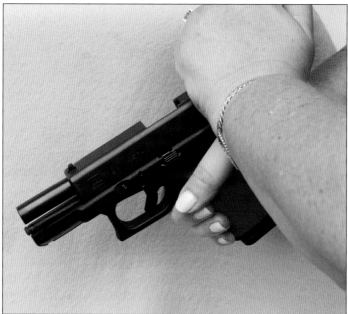

Figure 8-1. Tap, Rack, Reacquire

With a semi-automatic, the most common malfunction is a misfeed. The round fails to enter the chamber properly and the gun does not go into battery (ready to fire). You can see it: the slide is not all the way forward and the round is gleaming in the opening. This is usually the result of a "soft wrist," in other words not gripping quite hard enough. You do not need to white knuckle your pistol, but you should be gripping about as tightly as if you were squeezing orange juice. A soft wrist does not allow you to control the recoil and the gun will bounce a little, causing the failure. To clear a misfeed, remove the magazine and then rack the slide several times to release the round. Let it go—you do not want to take a chance that it was damaged when the slide came forward. Reinsert your magazine, rack the slide to chamber a round and keep shooting.

If you continue to have miss-feeds, you can ask an experienced shooter to try your gun. If they do not have any problems, tighten up the grip a little more and keep shooting. If your friend also has a misfeed, consider that it could be mechanical or ammunition-related. Try a few rounds from a different box of ammunition. Try a different magazine. Still no good? Field strip your pistol and look at the recoil spring. Can you compress it between two fingers without a lot of effort? It may be time for a new spring. Contact the manufacturer and they should be able to get you the correct part fairly quickly; and it is as easy to install as it was to take out, so you do not need a gunsmith. While you are waiting, do not risk shooting the gun. If you replace the spring and continue to have issues, then it is time to consult a gunsmith, but odds are you will have fixed the problem.

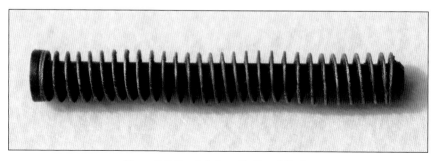

Figure 8-2. Semi-Automatic Recoil Spring

Another relatively common malfunction is a failure to eject the spent casing. Often you will see brass sticking up from the ejection port. This is called a *stove pipe*. Clear it as described above: tap, rack, and reacquire.

Figure 8-3. Stove Pipe Malfunction

Malfunctions of any kind are rare but they do happen. They can be caused by faulty ammunition, improper gun handling, mechanical issues, a dirty gun, and sometimes, it was just your turn. The key is to recognize the problem and know how to remedy it safely.

Chapter 9

PRACTICE, PRACTICE, PRACTICE

You have taken introductory training; you have bought your first gun, now it is time to *practice*!

Sometimes I go to the range for fun, sometimes I go there to work. Usually it is a combination of both. I am there to focus on improving a skill, but I have *fun* while I am there. I think of it as the Zen of Shooting. We have all experienced it. I go to the range, focus on my shooting and, when I'm done, I'm relaxed. All my stress, frustration, emails, phone calls, chores, work, deadlines have been shut out and by the time my hour is up I'm calm and relaxed and content, ready to return to my crazy world with a newfound sense of purpose and even serenity. Nothing else does that for me consistently the way shooting does.

Dry Fire

You need to read your owner's manual to ensure that *dry fire* is acceptable for your particular gun or if you need snap caps or dummy rounds (which are inert rounds that look similar to the real thing, but have no primer or power and have a plastic top instead of a bullet).

Figure 9-1. Dummy Rounds

They are used to protect the firing pin in some pistols. They are also great for practicing loading, unloading, and malfunction drills.

The recommended ratio of dry fire to live fire is 3 to 1. It helps you to hone your skills and focus on fundamentals such as trigger control. One way to challenge yourself is to place a coin on the end of your barrel and see if you can pull the trigger without dropping the coin.

To dry fire safely, you need a dedicated area to do so. You should always dry fire in the same place, so you become used to using it for that purpose. The number one rule is *no live ammunition* in the dry fire area—ever! You will need an effective backstop, just in case you violate rule number one. My basement is half-underground, with a cinderblock wall, and I have a Kevlar vest I can hang. That is my dry fire area. You can also use a brick or stone fireplace wall, a bookcase with lots of books (facing sideways) or you can get two 50-pound bags of sand and put them in a large pot or box. Another option is a Kevlar clipboard, available from www.thinkgeek.com for less than fifty dollars. It is small but I have had the joy of shooting one up at an outdoor range where it stopped a 9mm, a .38 and even shotgun home defense shot very effectively. The key is *always* triple check your gun to be sure it isn't loaded, then find, or create, a backstop that will stop a bullet, and minimize the amount of damage to property. Of course, if you unload, clear, check, check again and do not allow *any* ammunition in the area, you won't have any damage, but it is better to be safe.

Practicing at a Range

Practicing at a range is a classic way of increasing your shooting prowess. Start your target at 8 feet, get comfortable, and watch your grouping. Do not fall into the "Bang, where did I hit? Bang, where did I hit?" routine, where you shoot, then lower the gun to see where you hit. Fire several rounds and then look. When you are shooting well, move the target out to 12 feet, then 15, then 20, then 25. You can go farther if you want to, but if you are shooting for self-defense, it is unlikely that you will need to engage anything more than 10 feet away.

Practice makes perfect? *No!* Practice makes habit. I mentioned earlier that you must perform an action 1,000 times to make it a habit, and 2,000 times to break one. That sounds like a lot of work to me. I am lazy; I would rather learn it the right way the first time! Bottom line? Practice right! You are practicing your marksmanship, trying to hit the center of your target each time. Great goal. We all have off days, so be kind to yourself. Sometimes a nice tight grouping at 8 feet starts to spread out at 15 feet. How can you tell what you need to work on? Take another look at the fundamentals addressed earlier. You can also learn to read your target; it will tell you pretty much everything you need to know. The trick is trusting your eyes and correcting the issue. Right-handers, are you shooting center left of the bull's-eye? Try using less trigger finger. Left-handers shooting center right, same thing. Are you shooting low? You are probably anticipating the recoil and driving the gun down before the bullet has a chance to exit the barrel. Shooting high? You could be pushing too much on the grip of the gun (called heeling, as in the heel of your hand). Are your shots placed somewhat randomly? How is your trigger control—are you slapping or jerking the trigger instead of easing it straight to the rear and then riding it out to the reset?

Most modern pistols come from the factory with the sights aligned, so it is not likely that your sights are off. If you really think that might be the case, have an experienced shooter, or your instructor, take a few shots. If they are consistently off, in the same way you are, then it is time to visit an armorer or gunsmith. If not, refocus on sight picture and sight alignment, slow down, and try again. Sometimes I have to slow myself down, focus on the basics, get my confidence back, and keep shooting.

How you practice should mirror your plan for your firearm. If your focus is shooting for fun, you can stand in one place and plink away. If you want to use your firearm for personal defense, as you gain experience and accuracy, you can start to push yourself a little harder. Always check the range rules where you are shooting, but if it is allowed, you can try shooting with one hand, then the other. Yep, practice shooting with your nondominant hand just in case you are injured. Try kneeling or rolling around the shooting table. Note that your target should be lower so you are not shooting at an upward angle.

It might be ok to shoot slightly upward, but you do not want to hit the ceiling, or carriers, or to overshoot the berm (barrier) around the range. Try moving side to side, even one step. Just be careful to keep your pistol pointed down range and if you trip and lose your grip

Figure 9-2. Shooting Around a Barrier

never try to catch your pistol! Let it fall to the floor. Modern pistols are drop safe, meaning they will not go off accidently if dropped. However, if you try to catch it and accidently pull the trigger it will fire, and there is no guessing which way it will be pointed.

Next time you are practicing anything, ask yourself if you are doing it the right way. One reason this is so important is that, when shooting in an emergency, you will react as you have practiced. If you practice catching your magazine and putting it down before grabbing a fresh one to reload, what do you think you will do if your life is in danger? I have heard people say "I would never do that in a real-life situation." Sadly, many studies found police officers dead after a confrontation, with brass in their pockets. Why? When they went to the range, they would shoot (revolvers), catch the brass, and put it in their pockets so they would not have to pick it up later, and then reload. What happened in a real situation? They did exactly what they practiced. You need to practice for real-life confrontations, being aware so you aren't building "range habits" that can get in the way of your real-life response.

Do you catch your magazines when they are empty or do you let them fall? A magazine can be expensive, what if it breaks? Think about it: if it breaks from a drop, did you really want to trust your safety to it?

Do you use the slide lock to release your slide? Yep, that little button is a Slide *Lock* or Slide *Stop*, not a slide release. Why can that be a problem? Your slide may not come forward properly, resulting in a failure to go into battery, so the round may not feed correctly. When you rack the slide back, you pull the slide back a fraction of an inch, the extra distance, tiny as it is, can make a big difference. That is how your gun is designed to function. You don't get that extra fraction of an inch if you press the slide lock down. Also, that little piece of metal can break over time if used for something other than its intended purpose. Lastly, fine motor skills versus gross motor skills. Maneuvering tiny objects is a fine motor skill. What do you think is the first to go in a high stress situation?

Do you go to the range, practice a fast draw, fire three shots, and reholster? Ok, what is wrong with that you may be wondering? Step 1, fast draw—think *smooth* draw. Fast is slow, smooth is fast, minimize your movements. Watch the pros' economy of motion; they seem to be barely moving—everything flows and looks slow, but in reality they are super fast. Step 2, fire two, three or four shots (as long as you are on target and it is safe to do so). You want to vary the number of shots so you don't develop a habit of firing two and stopping, you may find yourself in a situation where you need to shoot three! Step 3, come to low ready and make the decision to reholster. *Low Ready* is when your gun is still pointed toward the threat but pulled in close to the body. When should you reholster? When you are sure the threat is over. Come to a low ready, assess, and then decide if it is safe to reholster. There are no points for putting your gun back in the holster fast. "Look," or watch as you put your gun back into the the holster to be sure it is going where you think it is. If you don't reholster until the threat is over, or until you've drilled a couple cycles on the range, then you don't have a reason to hurry. Practice at the range, draw, fire, reassess, maybe take a couple more shots, reassess, reholster. Next round, draw, aim and do not fire, maybe your target is running away. Next, draw, fire, reassess, fire, scan left and right, then over each shoulder, all from a low ready keeping your gun pointed squarely down range. Think about possible scenarios and practice the way you would use them in real life. Make the habit to draw while assessing, fire if appropriate, reassess.

Figure 9-3. Low Ready Position

Figure 9-4. Reholstering

Figure 9-5. Scanning for Danger

Reloading: Eventually your magazine will empty and your slide will lock back. Bring the gun into your high ready position, similar to your work space (revolvers are different, I'm referring to semi-automatics here), close to your body so it isn't easy for someone to grab. With whichever hand is your primary for that session (strong or weak) holding the gun in your one-handed grip, tilt it slightly so the mag well is angled toward the center of your body. Release the magazine and let it fall at the same time you are going for your spare magazine with the free hand.

Indexing: With your index finger along the front of the magazine, insert the mag into the mag well, pushing up until it clicks in. Give a slight tug to be sure it is seated, and rack the slide to chamber a round. Your eyes should be looking out toward any threat(s). You've practiced the reload, you can see it in peripheral vision or a quick

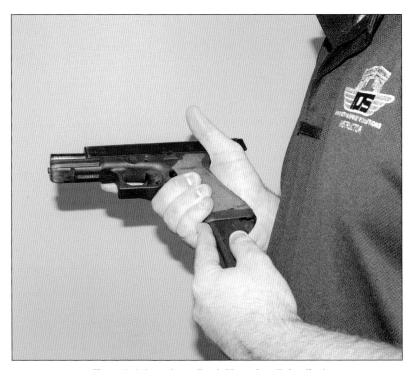

Figure 9-6. Inserting a Fresh Magazine (Reloading)

glance if needed. You do not need to watch the mag go in, you can feel it.

Do you own a *blue gun* (a plastic or wooden training pistol that is the same size and shape as the real gun it is modeled after but with no moveable parts) in the model of your carry gun? If not, you might want to consider it. I own three, actually. I have found them to be irreplaceable for training situations at home. Dry fire in a controlled environment is important, but there are things I want to practice

Figure 9-7. Glock 19 Blue Gun and Real Pistol

where I do not want to be in my controlled environment, which is quite limited.

I use my blue guns to try out holsters and to practice drawing. I play a game with my husband where I will be wearing a blue gun just like I would my carry gun and he will call out "Threat," and we will time how long it takes me to sweep my cover garment and draw.

It is one thing to practice a fast draw when you tell yourself in your head *now*, and quite another when someone else calls it out, even when you are expecting it. It has made a big improvement in my reaction time. I can roll on the floor; I can beat on my heavy bag, "escape" from it, and draw on the move. All in complete safety. I do not feel comfortable doing that with my real gun. Do not misunderstand, a blue gun is not a toy, it is a tool. For me, it is a tool to inject a little reality into my practice and help me build skills I hope I never have to use.

Practice Safe and Practice Smart!

Chapter 10

CLEANING YOUR GUN

Cleaning your gun can be fun, you get to take it apart, see the insides, and you have the satisfaction of doing it yourself. Make sure you have a cleaning kit that is sized to your caliber gun. The bare essentials include:

- A Bore Brush
- A Jag or Needle Threader
- A Cleaning Rod
- A Bristle Brush (similar to a toothbrush)
- Bore Cleaner
- Gun Oil
- Patches
- Eye Protection
- Latex Gloves
- A Soft Rag
- A Shot Glass or Small Glass Bowl

Every gun is a little different, so consult your owner's manual for specifics of how to break down, clean, and oil your particular gun.

Generally, for a semi-automatic, you will field strip it, or do a basic disassembly. If you have a revolver, you will simply open the cylinder. Before you start cleaning, you need to remove all ammunition and ensure the gun is unloaded. Check again! Redundancy is the mother of safety. Your loved one does not want you to be one of those headlines "Woman Accidentally Shoots Self While Cleaning Gun." It is shocking how often that happens.

Keep all ammunition away from the cleaning area. It can be damaged by the cleaning solvents. Plus, if it is there, you may accidentally, or absentmindedly, load your firearm. Once your cleaning area is secure, you can break down, or open, your pistol. This is a great time to see how it works, check for signs of wear, and generally get to know your gun. The better you know your gun, the more likely you will spot a problem early. I enjoy cleaning my guns; it makes me feel I am taking personal responsibility for my safety, and I can spot signs of wear early.

I recommend pouring a small amount of bore cleaner into your glass dish or shot glass. This is what you will use to clean your gun. When you are finished, you will throw the cleaning solution away. This avoids contaminating your bottle of bore cleaner with dirty tools. You do not want to pour it back in the bottle for the same reason. Make sure you keep your dish or glass with your cleaning kit (I store all of my components in a plastic ammo can) so that you do not accidentally use it for anything else.

Follow the specific instructions for your gun, but the basic steps include wetting a patch with bore cleaner and running it through the bore and the chambers in the cylinder of your revolver. Do not be surprised if it comes out black, it is cleaning away the lead and powder residue from inside your gun. Your patches and brushes should be sized to your particular gun, matching the caliber, so they will fit properly. The packages are all labeled, so you should easily find what you need.

Next you will run the bore brush through your bore, all the way, straight in and straight out. You can do this several times to scrape the gunk loose. Do not twist the brush as you risk scratching the

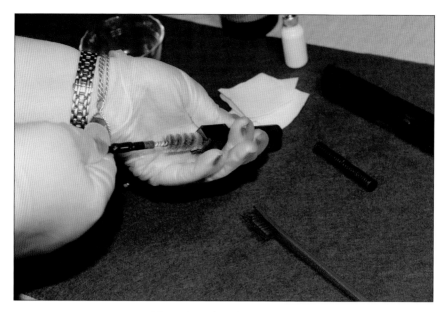

Figure 10-1. Cleaning the Bore

inside of the bore. You want to use a smooth controlled movement to avoid any accidental damage. If possible, insert your cleaning tools in the same direction the bullet travels. If you have a revolver or other firearm where the barrel does not detach from the frame, this won't be possible, but try to be gentle and as consistent in your cleaning as possible. As you get more comfortable cleaning your firearm, you will feel when it is clean. Next, you will run clean patches through to pick up any residue. Use each patch once and throw it way, get a clean one, and send it through. You will do this until the patch comes out clean.

You can dip the cleaning brush into the bore cleaner and use it to scrub the outside of the bore, the slide, the cylinder on the revolver, and any exposed parts that need to be cleaned. Next, using patches or a soft cloth, thoroughly wipe down all the surfaces to remove any trace of bore cleaner and lead or debris. Keep wiping until all the patches come away clean.

Next, you will add a little oil. Again, check your owner's manual. Some guns like very little oil, such as a Glock, while some want to be basted like a roasting turkey. Your owner's manual will tell you how much and where to apply the oil. A needle oiler, while not necessarily part of your bare essentials kit, can be very handy for the precise application of oil. Once you are done, wipe away excess oil with a clean patch.

Figure 10-2. Removing the Recoil Spring for Cleaning

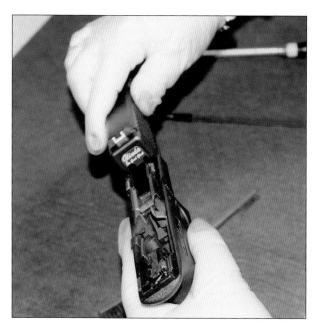

Figure 10-3. Reassembling Pistol

Now that your gun is clean, you can reassemble it, or close the cylinder. Dry fire a few times or rack the slide a few times to ensure all the parts are where they should be and everything is working. Then, give your gun a nice rubdown with a clean, soft cloth to remove any traces of oils, fingerprints, or errant debris so that it is clean and gleaming. There is a lot of satisfaction knowing that you can break down (or field strip), clean, and reassemble your gun. Since I'm trusting my life to it, I think it's important knowing how it works and that I can keep it clean and functional.

How often do you need to clean? Again, this varies by gun, and you can consult your owner's manual. I like to clean it more frequently than is suggested in the manual. If you just returned from a trip to the range and will be storing your gun for a month, clean it. If you will be returning to the range within a week, maybe you can wait. Some people like to see how many rounds they can put through a gun before issues arise from not cleaning it. These are usually men. If it is a range gun, ok, I may let it go a little longer. My carry gun, I clean after every trip that involved at least 200 rounds. I clean my .22 calibers every time I shoot them, no matter how few rounds. The rounds in a .22 tend to be a dirtier round because they generally have a lead tip that leaves more debris than a jacketed round. Bottom line, very few, if any, malfunctions have ever been attributed to a gun being too clean, but many can be attributed to a gun being too dirty. Also, malfunctions can happen due to too much lubricant. Check the owner's manual, ask the manufacturer, or talk to someone experienced with that particular make and model.

Chapter 11

STORING AND CARING FOR YOUR GUN

Part of being a responsible gun owner is protecting your gun from unauthorized access. If you have children in the home, do not make the mistake of thinking they do not know where the gun is. If you are like me, when you were a child you knew every hiding spot for the Christmas gifts and could find them, open them, and return them … undetected. Children are crafty! If you hide it, they will know. There is also a curiosity factor: if the gun is a "secret," kids will be curious. Unfortunately, this can lead to tragic accidents. This is the reason I strongly advocate teaching gun safety to kids if you have a firearm in the home. Even if you don't have one, they will know what to do if they are at a friend's home and discover a gun.

If you are keeping a gun for home defense, consider a small gun safe with a biometric or handprint combination lock that you can open in the dark. You do not want to be fumbling with keys or combination dials in an emergency. Many of these are now electric, with a backup power supply for outages. A large number of these will also temporarily lock out anyone who has entered the wrong combination a predetermined number of times, such as three. Additionally, some models have an indicator so that you know if someone has attempted access. Consider your situation and your budget to determine the level of security you need in your home. Also, if you have children in the home you should verify the requirements for your state; there may be special lock requirements.

If your household is adults only, you may still need to take precautions in the event you have visitors, whether adults or children. You must protect your gun from the innocent and the foolish.

If your firearm is not for home defense, locked storage is your safest option. If you are storing your gun between trips to the range, it should be unloaded. If possible, consider a felted gun case. Long-term storage in the egg crate foam cases can lead to rust! Store your ammunition separately from your gun. I keep mine in the factory boxes in a plastic ammo can with a desiccant, which is a chemical that removes moisture from the air (similar to the little packets that often come in new leather purses and shoes, except much larger). I also keep a desiccant in my safe with my papers and my guns. Your ammunition should be kept in the original boxes. There is a lot of good information there: the manufacturer, caliber, lot number. These can be important if you find you have malfunctions with a particular box. You can contact the manufacturer and ask if there was a known defect. Often they will replace your ammunition for free if there was a defect.

Your ammo should be kept away from water, solvents, and chemicals, any of which can cause degradation or damage. If the box shows signs of exposure to anything, do not take a chance. Take it to the dud box at the range for proper and safe disposal. Some people resist throwing away "good ammo," but is your firearm, your hand, or even your life worth the risk? If in doubt, throw it out.

Do not expose your ammunition to extreme temperature, such as storing in a hot or cold attic. Temperature extremes can also cause the powder to degrade and not function properly. It is always better to be safe; if there is any doubt about the ammunition, do not shoot it and dispose of it safely. As mentioned earlier, most ranges have a dud box and can safely dispose of damaged ammunition.

Chapter 12

PRACTICE VERSUS DEFENSIVE AMMUNITION

We discussed earlier the importance of finding the correct caliber and power ammunition for your firearm. Here we will address the difference between the type of ammunition we practice with versus what we carry, and why they are not the same.

The two main differences are price and function. *Practice rounds* are generally much less expensive; they usually have a solid rounded tip, or bullet, and will penetrate, or travel, farther than defensive ammunition. *Defensive ammo* is approximately 2.5 times the cost of practice rounds. The preferred defensive ammunition is hollow points. HPs, as they are sometimes called, had a bad reputation years ago as "cop killers," but they are designed to be safer for the innocents in a defensive situation. They are characterized by a depression, or divot, in the tip of the bullet, and are often scored on the sides. Some, such as Hornady Critical Defense, have a polymer or rubber tip inside the opening to support the mushroom or blossoming effect of the bullet upon impact. Many manufacturers sell HP rounds; you need to try the various rounds to see what you are comfortable with, what works well in your gun, and what gives you the best result for the price.

Figure 12-1. Remington 9mm Practice Round, Hornady 9mm Critical Defense Hollow Point and Magtech Guardian Gold HP 9mm

So, why not use the less expensive rounds for self-defense? The solid round-nose bullet will penetrate walls, or other barriers, and unchecked can travel distances up to a mile unless it encounters a sufficient backstop. A human body is not usually a sufficient back-stop. When shooting, for practice or defense, you must always be aware of what is behind your target. Both types of bullets may pene-trate your target, but the round nose will keep going, possibly with unintended consequences. This is fine for the range where you have a backstop to stop the bullet, but in a defensive situation, you could be putting anyone beyond your target at risk.

Not all hollow points are created equal. Look for a scored tip, meaning little grooves cut into the sides to help it expand and blossom out upon impact. The hollow-point bullet is designed to lose much of its velocity when it hits something. It will slow down and mushroom, or blossom, open, *minimizing* the risk beyond the target (but you are still responsible for knowing what is there, and that it is safe to the innocent for you to take your shot). A hollow point actually has more stopping power, in that as it blossoms out, it will do more damage, and if it exits the body the exit wound will likely be much larger than a round nose, which makes a small entry and exit wound. It could still penetrate your target, or a wall, but will be slowed significantly, and the diameter will have dramatically expanded.

You are responsible for ensuring that it is safe to shoot before you take the shot.

There are many places to buy your ammunition: a gun store, Wal-Mart, a sporting goods store, and many online resources that may offer a lower price, sometimes better pricing if you are buying multiple boxes. Examples include www.Cheaperthandirt.com and www.luckygunner.com. There are many more; ask your shooting buddies where they get their ammo, and you may be able to save yourself some money!

Chapter 13

NEXT STEPS

You have discovered the joy and fun of shooting! You've begun practicing, learning, honing your skills—now what? Consider taking additional classes as your funds permit. Go shooting with friends and challenge each other. Consider competing. Think about becoming an instructor! We need more passionate women instructors. There are NRA Instructor Certification classes available, and once certified, consider working with a training team so you have support and backup and shared responsibilities. There can be a lot of personal satisfaction in sharing and helping someone else discover the joy of shooting, helping them take that First Shot. I enjoy seeing smiles on the faces of the women when they realize they just shot a great grouping and had fun!

Always keep learning, consider joining a shooting league, enter some competitions, or independently work your way through the NRA Winchester Marksmanship Program, which reinforces the fundamentals and helps you work on new skills a little at a time. It is a self-paced program—the guidelines are available through the NRA. You start simple, and it gets harder as you progress, but it helped me to learn to shoot with either hand as well as hone some of my basic skills. I have also completed the Pistol course of fire, earning my Distinguished Expert rating (which allows me to wear a lapel pin, a fancy medal, and I have patches for each level sewn on a range bag). It wasn't easy and I learned a lot in the process, but with work I've discovered I could do it!

If you have the time, you can start your training to become a proficient markswoman, comfortable with handling your gun; then learn how to shoot for defense! There is a difference, which we will explore later in the book. Or you can start learning defensive skills and come back to the marksmanship. Both are important and the order is more up to you. But, and this is important, do not skip steps. Get comfortable with the basic skills, either defensive or marksmanship, or both simultaneously, before you move into the more advanced shooting. It is like learning to crawl before you walk, and learning to walk before you run.

Keep shooting and enjoy!

Figure 13-1. Defensive Shooting Student

Chapter 14

PHYSICAL LIMITATIONS DON'T HAVE TO STOP YOU FROM SHOOTING

Shooting is a sport that transcends gender, age, and most physical limitations. Young children shoot. Senior citizens shoot. Amputees shoot. Even blind people, with the help of a spotter, can and do shoot. I have seen photos of a man who shoots with his feet because he has no hands, and he shot better than many people with no such limitations.

If you can hold a gun and pull the trigger, you can shoot it. It may take patience, strengthening exercises, and creativity, but almost anyone, standing, sitting, or lying down, can shoot. I once worked with a student who had a pronounced tremor in his hands, but he learned to read his tremor to know when to pull the trigger. He has a very impressive shot grouping. I've had students who had carpal tunnel, who would be fine for a short time until it would become painful. It is ok to shoot for however long you are comfortable and then stop. Everyone's shooting experience at the range can be customized to his or her comfort level. Some people have wrist or shoulder conditions that limit their mobility, your instructor can help you to find a way to manage that is both safe and works for you. Arthritis in the hands is a common concern for those of us over thirty (wink). First, try hand strengthening exercises to get as much range of motion and strength as you can (check with your doctor first if you have a diagnosed condition). Then look at your choice of firearm. An 11-pound trigger pull, such as you find on some revolvers, might not be a good choice, but a 5.5-pound (such as a Glock) might be more manageable. If you have difficulty racking the slide, you can learn to rack it off a table, shoe, belt buckle—all with one hand. Don't try to shoot a caliber that causes you pain. A .40 caliber might be too much, but a 9mm might be quite manageable. Also, there are adaptations you can make to almost any gun. I would start with the grip. If it is stock, it is probably hard. I changed out the hard plastic grip on my revolver, on my own, for a softer grip made by Hogue. It was not much more difficult than changing a light bulb, actually. What a difference! I liked it so well I got a Hogue sleeve for

Figure 14-1. My pink Hogue sleeve on my Glock

my Glock. That was a little harder to get on. In theory it slips over the grip and provides extra cushioning. In reality, it is like fitting a size-16 body into size-10 jeans. But once it was on, it did add a little cushion and decreased the stress on my hand. It did not, however, make the grip look any slimmer.

Why am I sure this works? I have the aches, pains, and scars of someone who had an active "youth." I have also had carpal tunnel surgery on both hands, as well as various shoulder, back, neck, and knee injuries. The only thing that really slowed me down was breaking my wrist. It is very hard to shoot when you are in a cast. Ok, I couldn't use that hand at all, but once the cast was off and my wrist had a chance to regain strength, I was back at it.

You can do it! Find a caring instructor, use a little imagination, consult a professional to help, and you can find a way to overcome almost any obstacle or difficulty. There are also great websites with ideas, as well as information on the Paralympics shooting competitions that may give you some inspiration. Remember, little girls can shoot, octogenarians can shoot, *you* can shoot! You can sit, stand, or lie down. There is a way around almost any impediment you can think of. The key is to want to try, and then go do it!

Chapter 15

SITUATIONAL AWARENESS

Aware, Confident, and Safe!

As little girls, many of us were given dolls to mother and told not to play with our brother's toy guns. Young ladies don't yell, they don't hit, they are quiet, demure … I even wore white gloves and a hat to Sunday school. Ok, I may be giving away my age here, but truly, girls are generally raised differently than boys. We do not learn to fight, we learn to keep our discomfort hidden when someone invades our personal space or gets too friendly and gives us an odd feeling. This socialization, or conditioning, makes us ideal victims. We can be convinced that it isn't so bad, it is our fault for leading him on, we owe him, we are making too much of nothing, we need to keep our voices low. I lived the first thirty+ years of my life like that. Shy, reserved, passive—then I woke up. It took a traumatic event for me, but hopefully not for you. I still behave like a lady, but only when I want to.

What does this have to do with socialization? Ever get that uneasy feeling when someone crowds you in a checkout? It's ok to turn and politely tell them that you would appreciate it if they took a step back. This is very reasonable; they do not have any need to see your pin number, or your transaction total, or anything else that is *your* business. How often do we say something versus shifting uncomfortably and hoping they will get the message? What about the stranger approaching you in a dark parking garage, or lot, that just does not feel right. Do you ignore that feeling or look at him directly and tell him politely but firmly to stay back? Some people are innocently clueless of personal space. More often, they are testing you to see if you will tolerate the invasion. For some, that is a thrill, for others it is a prelude to something much worse. Do not give them the "in." You can be polite in an initial encounter, but also be firm. Leave no doubts that you mean what you say. These are forms of aggression, or small attacks, and they can escalate.

I recently had to ask someone to leave a meeting for being a disruption. I had already warned him several times, each time a little more forcefully. Finally, I stood up and told him he needed to leave since he was not able to control himself. He refused, I picked up my phone and dialed 911. He left, muttering profanities, but he left and did not return. I needed to escalate my warnings, and then back it up. I made eye contact, was polite but firm, and left no doubt that I meant it.

Sometimes you may wander into a situation without realizing it. If you are on someone else's territory, you may need to retreat. In those situations, an "excuse me, I am sorry for interrupting" and backing away can be enough. In other cases, you can use your gender to your advantage, as in "I am so sorry, I am lost, can you direct me to the nearest gas station?" or interstate, or whatever. Trust your gut on this. It can work in the right circumstance, such as accidentally wandering into a biker bar. Bottom line: get away from an uncomfortable situation fast.

You have the right to your space, your comfort, and your body. No one has the right to take that away from you. You can be feminine if that is what you want. You can be tough as nails, or you can be somewhere in between. However, you do not have to accept intimidation or aggressive behavior. Use your voice, stand up straight, make eye contact. No one can take your power from you without you giving it to him or her. You may have to dig deeply to find your inner strength, but it is there. Do whatever it takes to survive an encounter, be it eye contact, physically fighting back, or if you are mentally prepared and believe yourself to be in mortal danger, shooting your attacker. Remember, when someone attacks you, *they* have made the decision to do so. Your decision, your choice, is to accept it or fight back!

I have been told I project a "Don't mess with me!" attitude when I am walking. Some women are afraid that they appear less feminine that way, but I do not agree. I can project the same attitude in a skirt and four-inch heels as I can in my Tactical 5.11 pants and Firearms Instructor shirt. My husband actually finds it attractive. However, he also jokingly calls me his bodyguard. He knows I can take care of myself and that makes him more comfortable, but he also enjoys seeing me move with a sense of purpose and awareness. So, yes, I can be feminine and purposeful, even when I have to take smaller steps because my feet are killing me (but the shoes are so cute!). The attitude starts in your head; you decide that you are not going to volunteer for the role of victim. From there, you become more aware of how you stand, you automatically scan and become more aware of who is around you, and learn to make quick judgments of who might be a threat. Along with your posture is situational awareness, knowing what and who is around you. How do you know? Look around! Scan the area; are there tall shrubs that could hide an attacker? Is there a group of young men, or young women (girls can be just as dangerous, especially in groups)? Are they directly in your path? Maybe you should change direction. Do you walk through a parking lot with your head down, texting frantically like so many people we see these days? I actually had a young woman walk into the side of my car because she was texting and paying no attention to her surroundings. Are your arms full of packages and is your purse dangling as you make your way to your car, only to realize your keys are in the bottom of your bag? You cannot stop every attack, but you can take steps to not make yourself an easy target. Most stranger attackers will move on to someone who appears compliant and clue-less, if presented with someone who looks like they would resist, are aware of their surroundings, and will not be a compliant easy victim.

There are many things to be aware of. If you are in a parking lot, do you scan the area, looking between cars, watching the area around you? Do you see someone looking at you and then looking at a third person and back at you? You might be a target. Get out of there or be ready. Do you take advantage of reflective surfaces? You might see someone approaching by using the reflection in a car or store window. Do you face the ATM and stand close? Most ATMs now have mirrors on them, have you noticed that? Do you make eye contact with the person in line behind you to use the machine so they know you are aware of them? Attackers count on the element of surprise, they want to catch you off guard. If they know that you know they are there and you are paying attention, they may very well wait for a more compliant, and clueless, victim.

Figure 15-1. Using reflective surfaces

This tough looking man is actually my gentle neighbor who kindly offered to act the part of the aggressor for these photos. He definitely knows what he is doing, and because of that he knows how to avoid potentially dangerous situations.

Figure 15-2. ATM with mirrors

Remember it is not just men, or people dressed "thuggishly" who can be a threat. Women and well-dressed men can also be a threat. Sometimes people work in a mixed-gender team. Ted Bundy found great success by pretending to be injured and in need of assistance to lure his victims. You can always say *no*! It is never rude to protect yourself. If they had a bad intent, they may mutter expletives and move on. If they are sincere, they may be surprised, but that is ok. Reverse the situation. Would you rather someone deny your request for directions because they were uncomfortable or have them push down their fear and come to you? Still wondering? What if it were your sister, your daughter, or your best friend? You would want them to follow their instincts and protect themselves at the risk of being rude to a stranger. A common ploy is to ask someone the time. Simple, right? What do you do when someone asks you the time? Angle your wrist and look down to read your watch, thereby taking your focus off the stranger right in front of you? Or, do you bring your wrist up to where you can easily ready your watch and still keep focus on the stranger?

Lt. Col. Jeff Cooper was a combat veteran Marine and founder of the America Pistol Institute. One of his lasting contributions is the Cooper Color Code.

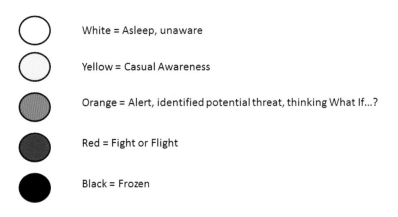

White = Asleep, unaware

Yellow = Casual Awareness

Orange = Alert, identified potential threat, thinking What If...?

Red = Fight or Flight

Black = Frozen

Figure 15-3. Cooper Color Code Chart

White is oblivious, asleep, completely unaware. Think of the person walking down the street, head down, texting away who steps off the curb and into traffic. They may be on the phone, listening to music, reading a book. What they share is a lack of situational awareness, and this makes them easy targets.

Yellow is aware, head up, confident, casually scanning your surroundings. You are not on high alert but you are aware of potential threats in your immediate area. It does not matter if you are ten or eighty years of age, projecting confidence in your walk and attitude can dramatically reduce your risk of an attack, or at the very least give you some warning that it is coming so you can prepare.

Condition **Orange** is when something catches your eye and you realize that it is not quite right. You may feel the hair on the back of your neck go up, or have an unsettled feeling in your stomach. Pay attention, something is off! It may be someone coming toward you. Flash mobs are a current danger, where a group of seemingly random people suddenly swarm together as a mob to wreak havoc. If you see people milling about and then they appear to catch each other's eyes and start to move together—get out fast! You may see someone paying a little too much attention to you, and then glancing toward another person; they may be a team, targeting you. You may sense someone is following you while you are driving. You are in Condition Orange; you have noticed a potential threat. Now, start thinking *what if ...* scenarios. What will I do if he suddenly starts toward me? What will I do if that random group starts to move together? What will I do when I notice that car behind me has been there for a while? Even if nothing happens, practicing the *what if...* helps you to begin to think about your response and keeping yourself safe. The more you practice *what if ...*, the easier and faster the response becomes.

Condition **Red** is the fight or flight stage. The threat is there, you must take action. You can move from Yellow to Orange to Red very quickly, but as you become used to being aware you will recognize situations that have the potential to turn bad, and you will begin to give yourself more time to prepare. Later we will discuss various options for the fight or flight response, but the key is recognizing and taking action, thereby avoiding Condition Black.

Condition **Black** is when you freeze. Time seems to stop, you cannot move, cannot think, and cannot respond. This happens to everyone at some point, but you must recognize it so you can shake it off and get back to response mode. Condition Black can be extremely dangerous, and very frightening. Just remember, it may feel like minutes but actually lasts only seconds; you need to push through so you can protect yourself.

Being aware, and using your brain, are the first steps to keeping yourself safe. Innocent victims are not dumb, but they are often naïve. They did not see the attack coming. They were not situationally aware. Keep your head up, your eyes open, and be aware. You will look more confident, more in control, and taller!

Figure 15-4. Being Aware of Your Surroundings

Chapter 16

BASICS OF UNARMED PERSONAL DEFENSE

What Is in Your Personal Defense Tool Kit?

What are the basic essentials you should have in your tool kit? For me, the first is situational awareness. If you do not know what is happening around you, you cannot respond to it! Second are the "what ifs," that process of thinking, if "X" happens, what I will do? I generally carry a flashlight, a kubaton, pepper spray, a knife, a whistle, and a gun. I also have a voice and I am not afraid of telling someone to *back off* in a way that lets him or her know that to keep coming is *not* a good idea.

What is in your basic tool kit? Start with your brain! Situational awareness is the key to anticipating, avoiding, and responding to a threat. What should you carry with you?

Flashlight. You can find a small keychain-sized flashlight at a grocery store, a hardware store, or a large mass retailer. I once found myself in a parking garage at night during a power outage.

I found my car without having to fumble in the dark. In a dark environment, a flashlight not only helps you to see where you are going, it can shine a light on someone who should not be there. You can also use a flashlight as a deterrent; you can flash the light in the eyes of someone who is a threat to you, rendering them temporarily blind by destroying their night vision and giving yourself time to get away. There are tactical flashlights, about the length of an ink pen, but with a larger diameter. They have the on/off switch at the rear of the flashlight, and usually a clip to make it easier to attach to a pocket. They may have a strobe function, and often a toothed bezel around the light to give you extra impact if you have to hit someone with it by driving it into their face or hand.

Pepper Spray. This is a nonlethal option to deter an attack. However, the laws vary from state to state, some require you to register your spray, some prohibit it altogether. Check the laws for your state to be sure you can have pepper spray. If you get a keychain canister, do not get lazy and leave it in your purse while walking to your car. Have it in your hand or your pocket so you can get to it fast! Quick, get your keys! How long did that take? Three to five seconds would be pretty fast. An average person can close a twenty-one-foot gap in under three seconds. Can you recognize a threat, find your keys, and deploy your pepper spray in under three seconds? Do you know how your spray works? Have you practiced the activation and safeties? Do you know if it is a stream, mist, or foam? Do you know how to decontaminate yourself if you are accidentally exposed?

SABRERed has the only formal civilian Pepper Spray training (Civilian Safety Awareness Program or CSAP) available as of this writing. If you cannot take a class, you should at least practice, in an open area outside away from people and pets and *not* on a windy day, to ensure that you know how your spray works and you have a sense of how to aim it to direct the spray into the eyes of your assailant. One caution, this is *nasty* stuff. When you are learning to use it, ensure that you point it away from your face, and not toward an innocent person or pet. If you are accidentally contaminated, flush the area with *cold* water for at least twenty minutes. You will not be happy, but it is temporary. Many people think *I'll use wasp spray,* or *I have bear spray for hiking, I can use that on an attacker.* If you read the canister, it usually carries a warning along the lines of: "It is a violation of federal law to use this product in any manner other than described." So, as much as you may want to "sting like a bee" you should stick with pepper spray and leave the house and garden chemicals for the nonhuman pests.

Defensive Posture. When someone comes toward you, it is a reflex to square off to this stranger, facing him or her. The hands come up in a protective gesture. Speak firmly and loudly, using as few words as possible. For example: "Get Back," "Stop," "Go Away," whatever words feel right to you. When I took the Pepper Spray class the first time, I called the instructor, who was playing the bad guy, "Dirt Bag." I was caught up in the moment; I actually like this person and felt bad later. Practice your commands until they are comfortable. Remember your social conditioning? We do not naturally bark instructions like a drill sergeant, but this is the image I want you to use. If they keep coming, draw your pepper spray and get ready. Keep your empty hand up to protect yourself and aim for the eyes. The effective range on most sprays is five to eight feet. A direct shot will temporarily blind your aggressor but his momentum may continue to carry him forward so you need to be somewhere else, to "get off the X" as my instructor likes to say. Move away from your current position, at an angle, as you are spraying so he cannot see where you are moving to.

Figure 16-1. Basic Defensive Posture

Figure 16-2. Getting off the "X"

One final note on pepper spray, some states require that pepper spray be registered, or have a minimum age to carry it. Check your local laws before you buy to ensure that you are acting within the law.

Another great item for personal protection is the simple *whistle*. Even if you panic and cannot get words out, if you can draw a breath, you can blow in a whistle, making noise, attracting attention and hopefully panicking your attacker. I keep one on my keychain.

The last item in our basic tool kit is a *cell phone*. It does not do much during an immediate threat but can work wonders right after. You can call for help if you are stuck somewhere, you can call the police, a friend, a taxi. Use yours to call the police immediately after an encounter. Tell them what happened, what you did, describe the aggressors, answer their questions—do not delay in making this call. The last thing you want is for the bad guy to call the police before you do and tell them there was a crazy lady in the parking lot yelling and making threats. You laugh, but it can take a lot of explaining if they come track you down. In addition, the sooner you call the better chance there is of finding the creep before someone else is hurt.

What is in your hand already? Are you carrying coffee? You can throw it in his face. This should distract him, giving you a chance to get away. Keys, they hurt when you hit someone with them. Is it a mugging or robbery? Throw cash, or your purse, away from you and go in the opposite direction. I know the thought of giving up your bag or wallet is hard, but everything in your purse can be replaced, you cannot. I carry my cash separate from my license and ATM card so I can throw my coin purse if I have to. If you can afford it, consider keeping a small stash of bills, maybe a lot of ones, in an easily accessible place in your purse that you can grab and throw. Chances are good he is more interested in the money than in you. Also, make a list of everything in your wallet, or photocopy the cards and identification you carry regularly, front and back, and store that in a safe place, just in case.

What about other things you might have available to you? If you are injured and using a cane or crutches you may look like an easy target. Take a few minutes to practice and get a feel for keeping your balance while using your cane or crutches to maintain distance from your attacker or to hit them. Thrusts can be effective and not adversely affect your balance. A cane can be used to punch and then swing like a bat. These techniques are best practiced, in slow motion, with great care to avoid additional injury.

Anything you do to distract your assailant gives you a chance to get away.

Okay, those are the basics, but what about when things become escalated and you need a weapon for protection? We will address an armed response later in this book, but here let us look at other options beyond the basic tool kit.

- Stun Gun. Effective, yes. However, you must be close enough to be in physical contact, and you must maintain contact for three to five seconds for the effects to occur. That can be a really long time in a scuffle. It is not likely that your attacker will comply meekly while you are doing this.
- Tasers are also quite effective; however, they take some skill to deploy effectively and since most are not easily "reloaded" it is not likely you will practice. In addition, the probes must be spaced apart, and penetrate to the skin, so if there is a heavy coat, or one misses—well, it is not going to help much.
- Knives take a lot of practice to use effectively. They are a close combat weapon, are not for the squeamish, and there is a real risk of having it taken away and used on you if you are not properly trained. Also, a folding knife may take time to deploy, open and use. The best defense is a fixed blade used for thrusting. However, understand that anytime a knife is used, the odds are someone, probably both the attacker and the victim will be injured.
- Kubaton. This also takes skill and training. It is essentially a stick, with or without a pointed end on it. There are many

things you can do with it, but it does take specialized training. I do carry one with my keys on the end. It makes my keys easier to find, and I can always swing it.

Physical Resistance

This is a big leap for most women. First, recognize that *you are important; your life is worth defending!* Second, remember, you did not start this. I have often said, "*I won't ever start something, but I will certainly finish it.*" What does that mean? Never give up! If you are hurt, scared, feeling helpless—do not give up, keep resisting with every ounce of strength and resolve you have; you are stronger than you know, and *you are worth it.* Keep going until the threat is over—maybe you won, maybe he ran away, maybe someone came along and scared him away. Do not go with him in the hope that you can get away later. There are no absolutes, but going to a secondary location often ends very badly; think about robberies where everyone is ordered into the back room, or the rapist who forces his victim to an isolated area where there aren't witnesses. Once he is no longer a threat you do have the obligation to stop your attack, or counterattack. If you continue once he is down, then you become the attacker and the law looks at you in a different way, so stop, escape to a safe place, and call the police.

Physical resistance is a learned skill. There are as many schools of thought as there are programs that teach it. Following is my personal philosophy. If you want to take formal training, I encourage you to search the Internet for Personal Defense training in your area. This is tailored more to street fighting, no rules, just surviving until you can get away. Martial Arts are great exercise but generally do not prepare you to defend yourself. In addition, if you (like me) are over forty and have your share of lingering aches and pains from pushing too hard in your younger years, martial arts can be daunting or impossible. I opted to take personalized one-on-one coaching in the Tony Blauer Spontaneous Protection Enabling Accelerated Response (SPEAR) program. I wanted to learn basic defensive techniques that I could do with my limitations, in the hope that I would never need them.

Women do not usually grow up learning to throw a punch. However, we can be very strong with an open hand. Try this exercise: have someone grab your arm and pull. What happened? Now, splay your fingers wide, tense your arm, and have the same person pull your arm. Notice a difference?

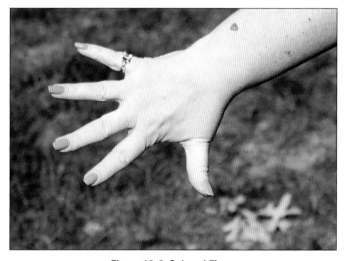

Figure 16-3. Splayed Fingers

Figure 16-4. Splayed Fingers equal strength and resistance

Your situational awareness should be on high alert when a potential threat is within striking distance. Watch them closely, they will telegraph their moves. For example, right before delivering a blow to the jaw, commonly called a "Haymaker" you may hear an intake of breath, you may see a narrowing of the eyes or a barring of the teeth. You will see the body rotate away from you slightly as the arm draws back and the hand forms a fist.

Figure 16-5. Incoming Haymaker

This all happens very fast, but if you are alert to it, you will see it and the foreknowledge can give you an advantage. You have spotted the signals, be ready, if it connects, it will *hurt*! Let your head rotate with the punch, do not try to resist, that makes it worse, and you could be seriously injured. The key is to react to what you see coming to avoid the impact. Remember the extra strength you felt with the open hand? Now is the time to use that to your advantage as you raise your arms to deflect the blow. Then turn into him, rolling through, as you push him back and off balance.

Figure 16-6. Deflecting the Haymaker

One of the most frightening scenarios is the grab from behind. If you are aware, you will sense someone approaching behind you. It could be a scrape of a shoe, it could be an intake of breath, a low growl sound, even a feeling in your gut, but you just know. This gives you a moment to start to respond. Raise your shoulders; this protects your neck if you are grabbed around the throat. If you have time, bring your hands up so that if you are grabbed in a bear hug your hands are on the inside of the clutch.

Figure 16-7. Neck Grab from Behind (Notice Shoulders)

Figure 16-8. Part-1 Bear Hug from Behind

Figure 16-8. Part-2 Bear Hug from Behind

Figure 16-8. Part-3 Bear Hug from Behind

Your focus is on getting him off you. The strongest places on a woman's body are the heel of her hand, the outside edge of her forearm, and her elbow and her knee. You can do a lot of damage and give yourself time to get away.

One of your top priorities, besides yelling your head off, is getting your hands free. Try standing a couple inches away from a wall; place your forearms, palms to elbows, flat on the wall, now lean in with your full body weight. Ok, push back. Not easy! You probably can't push him off you in that manner, either. Now, slide your arms straight up. It works! Same thing if you are trapped in a hold. You cannot push his arms away, but you can move yours up and free.

Once your arms are free, you have options. Rotate toward him, remember, you are still in a bear hug, you can't push him off you, you need to go on the offensive. Reach for his face with an open, claw-like hand. Land just above the eyes and rake down. Yes, you may be a little squeamish, but remember, to your knowledge, you are fighting for your life. Stick your fingers in his eyes and pull downward. Show him the same mercy he is showing you. Remember, he instigated this! Turn into him, pushing with the side of your forearm against the side of his neck to put him back and off balance. Put your whole

Figure 16-9. Arms against the wall

body into it, and really push, while turning in toward him, this will help to drive him off balance. You want him to fall so you have a chance to run. It does not matter if you are 95 pounds soaking wet, or 200 pounds. You are stronger than you know.

Figure 16-10. Face Rake

Figure 16-11. Forearm to Neck

Figure 16-12. Turning in to Push Him Off Balance

Figure 16-13. Driving Assailant to the Ground

You can also use your elbow to land a hit to the ribs or the jaw. Be aware of telegraphing your moves, which means giving him a clue of what you are about to do, such as drawing back for a hit, or being tentative in your initial strike, and keep your hands open with your fingers splayed to maximize your strength. Hitting with a closed fist is an easy way to break fingers and other small bones in your hand. You can land a hard blow, even without drawing back.

There are the classics that most of us know if you are grabbed from behind. If you can accurately judge where he is, you can try

Figure 16-14. Elbow Strike to Jaw

Figure 16-15. Elbow Strike to Ribs

stomping on the top of his foot. Not great if you are wearing sneakers, but it works wonders if you are wearing a hard sole shoe or high heels! The other classic is the shin rake where you kick back and rake your shoe down the front of his shin; again this works best with a hard sole or heel.

Figure 16-16. Foot Stomp

Figure 16-17. Shin Rake

Some recommend letting your body go slack, or "dead weight." The effectiveness of this will vary with size. Men tend to be stronger, so you could end up dangling by your neck and in a lot more trouble than before. This is a judgment call based on your situation. In most cases, it is probably not a good idea.

But what about the fancy kicks we have all seen on TV? Ah, if only it were true. Even if you have the flexibility of a Radio City Rockette and try to land a high kick, what do you do when he grabs your foot? Now what? You are on one foot, off balance, and he is in control.

If you are knocked to the ground, remember to bring your arms and knees up to protect yourself, almost into a fetal position. Your hands up by your face, elbows out to block, knees up and ready to help protect your more vulnerable midsection. You can twist your body to block an incoming blow and minimize the injury. If you get the chance to kick him, turn your foot sideways to maximize the surface area you are using to connect and minimize the risk of sliding off your target. You want to deliver a blow that will make him think twice about coming close. Sometimes, you just need to buy a few precious seconds before help comes along, or you have a chance to run.

Figure 16-18. On the Ground Defensive Posture

If you are on your back, you may have a chance to deliver a sharp, and potentially disabling, kick to the groin. Do not be tentative—he is trying to hurt you. You may also be in a position to deliver a sharp kick to his shin, or knee, potentially knocking him off balance and giving you a chance to get up and run. If you are kicking his leg, turn your foot sideways to deliver the maximum impact and minimize the risk of deflecting off his leg.

Figure 16-19. On the Ground Sideways Kick to the Shin

Like everything else, practice, practice, practice. I have a heavy bag in my back yard. Not only do I whale on it to release stress, I practice hitting it, kicking it, pushing it, and raking it. I also have been known to try various combinations of hits: standing, lying on the ground, to practice a hard strike, stepping back and then drawing my gun (blue gun), etc. Practice helps me build my skills and gives me more confidence if I ever need to use these skills.

The keys to protecting yourself are remaining alert, not giving up, and remembering that you have the right to defend yourself against an attack. You did not ask for this, you do not deserve it, and you should keep fighting until you win. The best fight is still the one you don't have. All the practice and training can save your life, but the only absolute protection is avoiding the fight altogether.

Chapter 17

MAKING THE DECISION TO CARRY A CONCEALED FIREARM

If you live in one of the states where you can legally obtain a Concealed Carry Permit, and the majority of states allow this now, although the laws vary widely from state to state, you have a choice to make. To apply or not to apply? If your state allows it, I would suggest you apply. It does not mean you have to use it if you have it, but at the very least, it will make trips to the range easier for you logistically.

Generally the states are either "Shall Issue," "May Issue" or "We do not allow concealed carry." If you live in one of the few remaining states that do not allow concealed carry, or a jurisdiction within a state that does not allow concealed carry, you do have the option to apply for a nonresident concealed carry permit, from a state like Utah or Florida. You will need to complete a special class to do so, and that will let you carry in one of the states that recognize that permit. However, you would still be out of luck in your home state. An easy web search on Utah or Florida Nonresident Concealed Carry Permit will help you find the appropriate documentation and class. If you are in a "May Issue" state, you will probably need to provide justification for your request for a permit. Again, not all states are the same, some consider personal defense an adequate reason, some use the "May" to deny all permit applications. A "Shall Issue" state will grant your permit unless they find a valid legal reason not to, such as a criminal record, existing restraining order, etc. How do you know where you are? Do a web search on your state and concealed carry permit. This will help you find not only what the current law is in your state, but how to apply. Many states require some verification of formal firearms training; this could be a certificate of completion from a basic firearms class, or if you are former military many states now accept a DD214. Some states, or counties, require fingerprinting, and you may need to make arrangements with the local police or sheriff to get them. I'm not going into details here because the laws in each state change almost annually. A state that doesn't issue permits today may be a state that allows its citizens to carry next year.

Once you have a permit, the decision to carry takes on a completely new meaning. It is not an easy decision for most of us. The key question is could you use your firearm to defend yourself? Alternatively, and more bluntly, could you shoot someone if you needed to? If you have trouble with this question, you are not alone. Ask a random sample of fifty women, who are not already carrying concealed but are not strongly anti-gun, and approximately forty-five will say "absolutely" when asked if they could use a gun to defend their children. Maybe half will say yes to defending themselves. Don't your children deserve a mom who is there for them?

There are moral issues as well as religious and personal concerns when you ask yourself the question of could you shoot and possibly kill another human being. There are also potential criminal and civil legal liabilities. This is not a decision we make lightly, but it is a decision you must make before you holster your gun and walk out the door the first time, or even before you store a gun in your nightstand.

I will never shoot someone with the intent to kill them. I will do everything in my power to avoid a confrontation. If everything fails and I am in a fight for my life, I will know it was the assailant's choice to keep coming and I will do everything necessary to defend my life and stop the threat. If drawing my gun gives him or her pause and they turn and flee, I have stopped the threat. If I have to shoot them, I will, until they stop coming or surrender, and are no longer a threat to my life or my family.

There are key components to a threat: intent, means, and opportunity. All three must be present to justify the use of deadly force (and you may still be at the mercy of the justice and civil court system). I would rather defend my life and explain my decision later.

Intent is an overt act or statement that clearly lets you know that the assailant intends to cause grave injury or death, as in "I'm going to kill you" or "I'm going to pound you into tomorrow."

Means refers to the capability to carry out the intent. They may be armed, may have a physical advantage such as being larger and/or physically stronger than you are. They may be brandishing a weapon of some sort, a knife, a bat, etc. I was once approached by a landscaper who objected to me asking him to move his truck (which was blocking four parking spaces). Before he started toward me he reached into a bag and grabbed a trowel. I took off and the confrontation was avoided. But in that case, a simple garden tool could have been a serious weapon.

Opportunity is the ability to reach you before you can get away.

You need to believe, and be able to explain, why you felt threatened, how you felt threatened, and why you took the actions that you did and why you could not get away.

Stand your ground laws aside, the best fight is the one that never happens. However, if you are forced into a situation where you need to defend yourself and you are forced to pull the trigger, remember, two lives will be changed forever. If you cannot look yourself in the mirror and say, without hesitation, that your life is valuable and you have the right to defend yourself, *do not* carry a firearm. When the unthinkable happens, you will not have time to make that decision. You need to make the decision before something bad happens (which we all hope never will). It is ok not to carry; it is a deeply personal decision.

A gun is not a rabbit's foot or a four-leaf clover. Simply having it does not make you less vulnerable. In fact, if you choose to carry, you will probably find yourself behaving more responsibly, shrugging off slights and insults because you do not want to provoke or escalate a confrontation.

If you carry, when should you? Whenever it is legal to do so. If you only carry when you are going somewhere that you think you might need it, why would you go there? I would prefer to stay home. Incidents usually happen when we are not expecting them. I would rather have the option to respond. Having your gun gives you one more option.

Laws vary from state to state, but some are common. You cannot carry in a federal building, including post offices, courthouses, an airport security area, or anywhere it is posted NO FIREARMS. Know the laws for your state, and keep up with them, they change frequently.

Chapter 18

HOLSTERS AND DRESSING TO CARRY CONCEALED

Holsters, IWB, OWB, SOB?

Holster Mania the condition where you have more holsters than guns and most of them are in a bag or box. For most of us, we find our holster via trial and error. Some people like Kydex, which is a thermoplastic acrylic that can be molded into a shape and is quite durable, some like leather, some like a combination of the two. Some even prefer the reinforced rip stop fabric. There is Inside the Waistband (IWB), Outside the Waistband (OWB), Small of the Back (SOB), Strong Side, Cross Draw, Ankle, Shoulder, Thigh, and Bra … the list goes on. However, once you find that one holster that fits, feels good, works well with clothes, it is recommended that you train and carry in the same way as much as possible, if not 100 percent of the time.

Why? Imagine if you train and usually carry strong side hip. One day you go out and decide that based on what you are wearing that day you need to carry in a cross draw, inside the waistband, position. That day, you find yourself in a situation where you suddenly need your firearm. Where will your hand go? To your usual place, the strong side hip. There you are, fumbling to find your gun. In the interim, you have lost precious seconds, telegraphed to the threat that you are going for a defensive tool of some sort, so he (or she) knows you may be armed and might be using those precious seconds to close in on you.

Hence, the Holster Bag. If only we could do a swap meet for holsters! They are expensive so we do not want to toss them. So how do you find your perfect holster? That is a tough question. If you are lucky, you can take a concealed carry class where you can try on several different types and get a feel for what is comfortable. If not, you may need to try different holsters until you find "the one." If you can, ask other women shooters what they like, especially if you meet someone with a similar body type and manner of dress. Your instructor may also be able to offer some ideas.

Figure 18-1. Sampling from My Holster Bag

What is the purpose of a holster? To hold your gun! If it cannot do that, it is not any good to you. The first, and most important, consideration is it *must* fit your gun! Generic holsters do not provide good retention without a strap of some sort, which is one more thing you need to defeat to draw your gun. How do you normally dress? There are many things to consider when choosing a holster. Inside the waistband, outside the waistband, with one metal clip or two, with belt loops, the list goes on. The package says it fits your specific model, but can you take it out of the package and look at it? Ask if you can try your gun (unloaded of course) or borrow one from the gun store to try in the holster. Over a soft surface, like a padded rifle case, turn the holster upside down. Does the gun fall out? Give it a little shake. Still there? That is a good start! If it has adjustable retention, you can adjust the fit a little. If you ordered it online, try it over your bed with an unloaded, and checked twice, gun. Stayed in the holster? Great first step. Does the holster completely cover the trigger guard? Can you get your shooting grip with your strong hand

Figure 18-2. Holster Should Cover the Trigger Guard and Hold Your Gun.

while the gun is in the holster? All are important factors in choosing your holster.

Next, try it on. You might need to buy it to do that. Get a feel for it. Does it poke you in strange places? Can you reach it comfortably? If it has a sharp edge, you might be able to file it down a little. Can you sit down while wearing it? Sometimes the trick is to raid someone else's holster bag and try some on. Do not get discouraged, the perfect holster for you is out there; sometimes you have to look at a few to find it. You can also ask your instructor and friends who carry. Just remember, what is perfect for me may not be perfect for you. Holsters are a bit like shoes. Some pinch, some are too big, some are just uncomfortable, and some are just right! I generally carry a Desantisis Hybrid (kydex and leather, IWB, with big clips on it that I can run a belt through.

One exception to the rules above, the Remora holster. It looks very much like a pocket holster, and you can get one that has a Velcro flap that allows it to be attached OWB, but generally they tuck into a waistband, or you get the customization to use it as an Ankle or Thigh holster. I do not know what the outside fabric is composed of; however, it clings to your skin, gently but firmly. Your waistband doesn't need to dig in like a girdle to hold it in place, and once there, until you release the pressure, it isn't going anywhere. I've carried successfully in a broomstick skirt with a drawstring waist. As for the thigh option, it is only available for the smallish guns, but I've carried a Ruger LC9 quite happily under my skirt with no one the wiser. I like that the strap is long enough to wrap comfortably around a thigh that is closer to the waist measurement I had at eighteen. It stayed in place, didn't dig in, didn't shift around—not my first choice for carry, since I can't strap a Glock 19 to my leg, but I really like it when I'm in a dress. In a skirt, I can tuck the 19 into my waistband in a Remora holster. They are also somewhat customizable. Following directions from the company I warmed mine with my blow-dryer (I stuck the nozzle in the opening for several seconds until the fabric started to warm up, gently wrapped my unloaded gun in a thin layer of fabric, inserted it into the pouch, came back the next day and it was fitted to my gun perfectly. Easy to draw and reholster. Just be careful you don't drop it when you undo your waistband, especially in the restroom, if you are lucky it could end up on the floor, but if not you may have to go fishing.

You also need magazine pouches. Yes, you should always carry at least one spare magazine. My instructor tells the story of an off duty police officer who made a quick trip to a convenience store (a.k.a. Stop and Rob) for milk, carrying his off duty firearm. When he pulled up in front of the store, he looked in and saw someone holding a gun on the clerk, robbing the store. He recognized him as he has arrested him before. At that moment the robber glanced out the door, saw the cop and recognized him as someone who had arrested him before. He fired one shot at the officer who was exiting his vehicle. The officer returned fire with one shot and the robber fled. In the ensuing investigation it was noted that the officer's gun did not have a magazine in it. It was later found—under the car. Apparently, he had bumped the release getting out of the car and the magazine fell without him noticing. He was able to fire because he had one round in the chamber. But, he did not have a spare magazine. Had a gunfight ensued, he would have been in very serious trouble. The moral of the story, always carry a spare magazine! Mag pouches come in various sizes and styles, in various materials, just like holsters. The thing to remember is to look for ones that fit your magazines (single or double stack, caliber) and your carry style. Some clip on a belt, some have integrated loops, and Remora also makes tuckable mag pouches. These are great, especially for smaller magazines, such as for my LC9 that I thigh carry as I can tuck in a mag and slip it under my arm into the side of my bra. There the ammo is protected and accessible, and since it is the same material it doesn't move.

Carrying in Your Purse versus a Carry Purse

First, I do not advocate off-body carry as a primary method of concealed carry. However, I do understand that there are some occasions where carrying off-body might be preferred. The more I have studied this topic, the more TV and movies make me crazy. The woman walking down the dark street who suddenly turns and pulls a gun out of her purse and aims at the man approaching her menacingly. Charlie's Angels (the original), where they pull revolvers out of tiny purses. Ladies, be honest, how long does it take to find your keys? Five seconds? Ten seconds? Longer? Have to dump your bag upside down to find them? If you can find your keys in less than ten seconds, you are doing great! Now, how long will it take to find your gun in your purse? It is probably the heaviest item in there so it will be at the bottom. How will it be oriented? Will you have to fumble around to get the grip in your hand, pushing aside your wallet, compact, brush, cell phone and the like. What will be in the barrel? Oh, there is that pen I was looking for! Or, what about the trigger guard? Oops, found my lipstick! How many times will you muzzle yourself while trying to get a proper grip and orientation? If you are really good and can find, clear, and draw in under ten seconds, is that good enough?

A young, healthy aggressor can close twenty feet in two and a half seconds or less. If you did not see him coming, you really cannot ask him to wait to attack you: "Excuse me, I have a gun in my purse, would you mind terribly not knocking me senseless while I look for it? Thank you so much." What do you think will happen?

A concealed carry purse has a dedicated area for your gun, with a holster to help maintain its proper orientation. You always know where your gun is, how it is oriented and you can get to it, with practice, in two seconds or less. Gun purses are available from a variety of sources, including USGlaco, Gun Totten Mamas, Midway USA, even Amazon. If you must carry your gun in a purse, please use a purse designed to secure and carry your firearm.

There are risks to carrying in a purse. First, purse snatchers! They get not only your bag but also your gun! If you go anywhere, you must maintain control of your bag at all times. If you are a victim of a purse snatching, you risk losing your gun and arming a criminal. Don't think that carrying a gun will help you in a purse snatching, as they tend to be quick and unexpected. However, many concealed carry purses have adjustable straps that are long enough for cross body carry, and have a wire cable sewn into the leather to prevent the strap from being sliced. They make great commuter bags; even when I cannot carry (when I cross state lines to go to work into a state that does not allow carry) I often use a concealed carry purse on the subway to minimize the risk of losing my handbag.

Yes, you must be aware of the innocent, the young, the foolish, and the evil. You cannot hang it on the back of a chair, tuck it under the table to go dance, set it on the floor in a friend's home. It is your responsibility to safeguard your gun. If you must carry off-body, remember that you are responsible for your safety, the safety of those around you, and the security of your gun. I have a couple carry purses, but I use them very rarely. When I go to the doctor's office and I know there is a chance I'll be sitting on the table wearing last week's sports section, rather than try to remove and stash my gun, I will use a purse. Ok, for those wondering why I would carry in a doctor's office, why not? I do not carry because I think I might need it, I carry—period. I have never been good at precognition, if I was I could know when I would be in a dangerous situation and not go there. However, I do not know, so I like to be prepared.

Figure 18-3. Drawing from a Concealed Carry Purse

Yes, ladies, you can be armed and stylish at the same time.

Dresses are tough, but for a special occasion, you can consider a thigh band for a small pistol (it will not work well with a full-sized pistol as they weigh too much). If you do not like thigh-high stockings, or plan to wear pantyhose, the thigh band can be tricky. Some bands have a strap that goes around your waist, almost like a garter belt, to help hold it up. This can create some real issues when it is time to visit the Ladies Room. Remora makes a thigh holster that I have tried and *love*. It doesn't slide down, it is versatile as the strap Velcros on so you can take it off and use it as a pocket holster or in the waist-band. Flashbang also makes an interesting assortment of holsters for women that are made to attach to a bra, either in front or on the side under your arm. It takes a little creativity to find the right top, but imagine the bad guy's surprise when you reach up under your top, he is thinking va-va-voom, and instead you pull out a gun!

I prefer two-piece anything. Suits, slacks and a jacket, jeans and a sweater, even a belted dress with a jacket can work if you use a holster that fits your belt (keep in mind the belt must be substantial enough to support the weight of the gun (½-inch wide won't do it). Some manufacturers make tapered/contoured belts that support a gun and look more stylish from the front. When you lay it flat, it is slightly curved and the ends are narrower. However, you can expect to pay up to $100 or more for a good leather gun belt. I bought one that was two sizes larger than my waist, took it to the shoe repair shop and had them punch in a few extra holes. This left room for my holster and it works high on my waist, or lower on my hips, depending on my outfit. Again, as described above, the Remora is a viable option for carry when you have a waistband with at least some tension.

What are the secrets to effective concealed carry? First, get used to it! If you are fidgeting, adjusting your pistol, constantly checking it, people will notice. If you seem unaware of it, most people will never see it or will assume that lump is a cell phone. Being able to discern the outline of your gun is called "printing" and is frowned upon. Concealed means concealed—not seen. Below are a few fashion rules:

- Prints hide better than solids.
- Dark colors hide better than light colors.
- Side ruching (gathers) is your friend.
- Layers, especially if the outer layer is a little loose or flowing, hide very well.
- A jacket, open shirt, vest, cardigan, etc., are all effective camouflage.

- Nothing too tight so that it outlines the pistol, unless you have a looser cover garment over the top. This can give you the illusion of snug, body conscious clothing, while still masking your gun.

When you are assembling your outfits, think loose over snug. Show off your shape if you want to, and still conceal your firearm.

With a little creativity, and a good look in a mirror, you can be stylish, and armed. Do not rely on asking your significant other if they can see it. They know it is there and will be looking for it. Also,

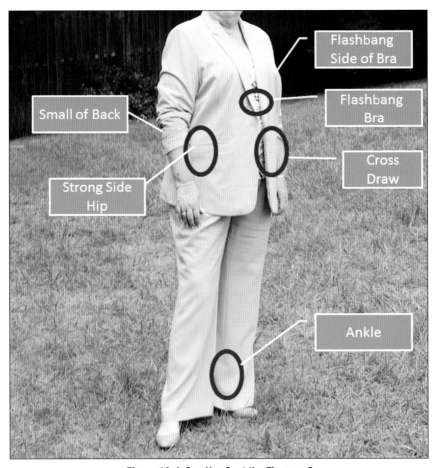

Figure 18-4. Can You Spot the Firearms?

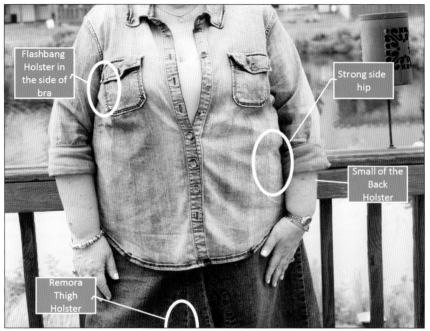

Figure 18-5. Can You Spot the Firearms? Part II

men, if she happens to ask, "Does this gun make my butt look big?" the only response is "Of course not, dear!"

Learning to wear a gun is like learning to wear a bra!

Remember when you were first learning to wear a bra? It was uncomfortable, constricting, the straps kept slipping, the band was irritating. I remember thinking I hated it and would never get used to it! Well, I did, as do we all, and now feel strange without one (of course, that could be due to ample proportions and gravity). Learning to be comfortable with your gun is the same thing. At first, it digs in, you bump it, you feel like it is sticking out a foot from your body and that everyone is staring at the lump under your clothes. You may feel the urge to adjust it and check it often. Then, one day, you realize, you are carrying your gun and you do not even notice it; you may not be comfortable but you are used to it. Comfort does come eventually. Just like a bra, you barely notice it is there and find you miss it when it is not. You realize that if people are staring it is because you are fabulous, not because you are armed. The lump, if noted at all, is assumed to be a cell phone or keys.

Like everything else, it takes time to become comfortable, so be patient. Of course, you have shopped carefully for a holster designed to fit your gun, and know that you have a secure fit and easy access. So relax and wear your gun in safety and comfort.

Once you have made the decision to carry and done your holster shopping and testing, how do you hide it? I prefer Inside the Waistband (IWB), which means the holster and gun are inside my pants or skirt, and there may be a clip, or clips, that extend over my waistband to hold it secure to my belt, or it is tucked into my waistband. Now, this means I cannot carry in a super-tight anything (as in jeans so tight I have to lay down on the bed and suck in my tummy to zip them), but snug works! I carry in my snug skinny jeans, a pencil skirt, and more. Ladies, if you find that jeans are a problem, the waist is too small when it fits everywhere else, consider men's jeans. You can buy them to fit your hips and have a little extra room in the waist. It is less expensive than alterations. I actually wear men's Tactical Pants when I teach because of the fit, and the pockets, but mostly the fit.

According to my tape measure, I am an "hourglass" shape, but I am also "plus-sized." It may be counterintuitive, but my curves actually seem to make carrying strong side (the same side as my dominant hand) hip easier. I carry on my hip, almost in a direct line with my arm, or side seam. The barrel is in line with my arm and my elbow rests on the grip of my gun. I carry a midsized 9mm semi-automatic. It tucks in nicely to my curves and all but disappears under most clothing. Some authors recommend appendix carry for women: this is slightly forward of the hip, aligned between the arm and breast (vertically speaking). I tried that and did not find it comfortable. It may be perfect for some, but not for me. I also found an ample chest interfered with my draw from appendix position. You need to experiment and find what is comfortable and what works best for you. For personal defense carry, you need fast, smooth access. That requires not only a good position but also lots of practice.

There are many other options such as on the belt, shoulder, cross draw (worn opposite the strong side), middle of the back, ankle, thigh, off body. All of these might work well for your backup gun, if you carry a second gun, but I wouldn't recommend them for your primary carry as they take more time to access. When fractions of seconds can make the difference between being a victim and being a survivor, you need to be able to get to your gun, draw, and acquire your target, safely and quickly.

Carrying Concealed When You Are Pregnant

Most of us understand that going to the range while you are expecting is probably not a great idea. The lead, the noise, none of it is good for the baby. However, as your tummy grows, your center of balance is shifted, and you may feel more vulnerable and want to continue to carry concealed, but how?

After a lot of thought, and asking several women who have young kids, we all came to the same conclusion, a Remora holster. Once you move from "regular" clothing to that with a stretchy panel, there is no belt to secure a holster, so you need something you can tuck into the general area of the strong side hip, shifting for comfort and the movement of your baby. If you are wearing a dress, your options are more limited, especially the closer you are to your due date as you probably can't see your feet, let alone reach your thigh. At that point you might consider a sized-up Belly Band (the stretchy band with the pockets for magazines and your gun). Wear it like a maternity belt, wrapped low under your belly. Yes, you run the risk of showing the world your Tuesday panties on Thursday if you have to draw, but it is better than being without your gun.

Chapter 19

INSIDE OR OUTSIDE

Keeping Your Family Safe

Does your family have a plan for what to do in an emergency like a fire or severe weather? What about how to contact one another in the event of a natural or man-made disaster when you are not all in one place? I live in the Northern Virginia area, and a lot of families were scrambling to contact each other, coordinate picking up kids, and so forth on September 11, 2001. Our cell towers were jammed, calls wouldn't go through. Storms, excessive call volume, even the authorities can bring down cellular service. Wouldn't you be more comfortable if you had worked out the details in advance? Do you have a safe room in your home and a plan for how to use it in the event of a break-in? Can you gather your family members together and protect them from an intruder?

Planning ahead, and practicing your plan, is the key to successfully keeping your family safe. Your safe room, often the master bedroom but it may vary depending on the layout of your home, can be your safe haven in an emergency. You should have your minimum tool kit available, a cell phone (if you get reception in your home), a hard line phone (not a wireless that will not be active during a power outage), your gun and ammunition. Another good idea is a spare house key on a bright and weighty keychain, something you can throw out the window to the police so they can enter your home without breaking the door. If your safe room is on an upper floor, consider a Fire Escape ladder. They have hooks that fit over the windowsill and rungs that unfold to offer you a means to escape. I found one at a major hardware store, from Kidde, for under thirty dollars.

If you can, consider replacing the standard interior hollow core door with a solid wood door that is more substantial and add a dead-bolt lock to secure it. If you cannot afford it, or are renting, consider a door security bar. Adjustable steel brace bars can be found for around twenty dollars. You can also cut a piece of 2x4 to fit the measurements you need. If you have a typical interior doorknob, you will want to put the brace against the bottom of the door and wedge it against something heavy like the bed, or a heavy dresser. This can slow down or prevent access to the room.

Do you have any cover if an intruder comes for you? A heavy wooden chest of drawers full of clothes pressed up against the interior wall between you and the hall may offer protection from a round fired through the wall. It may not stop it but it will certainly slow it down enough to reduce the risk.

Call the police and stay on the phone, even if you simply lay the phone down, the line is open, and the call is being recorded. This can provide evidence for you later. In your firmest voice yell out to the intruder that you have called the police, you are armed, and they need to leave *now*! If it is an innocent, such as a family member sneaking in late, they will be yelling back "Mom, it's *me!!!*" I've heard those words from my daughter who caught me by surprise late one night. She had forgotten to call out when she entered the house, she never forgot again! But, that is a whole other situation that we will not go into any further here.

If possible, stay in your safe room until the police have arrived and cleared your home to ensure no one is there who should not be.

Your connection to the arriving officers is the 911 operator. You can communicate how many of you there are, your descriptions, that you are armed and where in the home you are. The operator can communicate when the officers will be on site and what their names are. If a voice calls to you from the other side of the door and says they are the police so it is ok to open the door, *do not do it*! Ask them for a name and confirm it with the 911 operator. Bad guys are sneaky and they know all the tricks.

Under no circumstances should you meet the police with a gun in your hand. They are responding to a call, their adrenaline is high because they do not know what they are walking into. Do not be mistaken for a threat by putting yourself in the position to create a tragic accident.

Remember, your property can be replaced, you cannot. Do everything possible to avoid a confrontation with an intruder in your home.

What if you are outside your home with your family? If you are confronted by a threat, you want to have a plan so the threat is focused on you, not them, and you want distance between the threat and your loved ones so you can focus on what you need to do. This can apply to friends that you go out with routinely as well. Do you have girlfriends you walk with on a regular basis? Shop with? Talk about a plan in case something happens. Your family or friends need to move away from you, at an angle, preferably to cover, and stay there, calling the police, until the danger is over. As you walk, you can practice identifying cover, something that will offer protection as well as hide you. Concealment is your second choice as it will hide you but not stop a bullet.

When I first had this discussion with my husband, I asked him where he would go if we were confronted and I had to draw my gun? His initial response was to get behind me, thinking he would still be close enough to back me up if needed. A lot of people have a similar response: I'll get behind my friend or significant other. I also had to pose the tough question. If we are confronted by an armed aggressor, and I'm the only one of the two of us who is armed, how much backup can you really give me? Behind me is not a good place to be. For one, it keeps him in direct line with the threat while potentially limiting my movements. If I have to back up then I need to be careful that I'm not tripping on him. I will have a split focus when I need to be 100 percent focused on the threat. I need him away and safe so I'm not worried about him, I'm defending us directly. I want him behind cover calling 911. He had some trouble with that at first, as most spouses do, but understands the logic. Lately, we've had some issues in our community. Remember Intent, Means, and Opportunity? If we are on a Neighborhood Watch patrol and attacked by an unarmed woman, if he hits her, odds are it will be an assault and an arrest charge. If I intervene, it is more likely self-defense. If we are attacked by a man, it is a different story. Gender factors into the Means portion of the equation.

In a parking lot, hopefully you have had time to prepare because you identified the threat early on. Can you get a physical barrier between you and the threat? A car, a shopping cart? Use whatever is handy to give yourself an edge.

Are you driving and notice someone who appears to be following you? Make a right turn. Are they still there? Make another right turn. Still there? Ok, time to put your plan into action. Your first instinct may be to race home, but that is the worst thing you can do as you are leading them to your home. Instead, drive to a bright, populated area like a gas station, fast food restaurant, or shopping center and hit the horn. Attract as much attention as possible to get help.

You can teach your children about safety without frightening them. Make it a game for them, as in we are practicing our Safe Drill today. When you are out walking, call out "Cover" and have them run to what they think will provide cover. Were they right? Great, if not, explain why. Call out "Conceal" and have them hide somewhere. Let them know when they get it right. At home, you can practice your safe drill, gather everyone into the safe room and place them where you want them to be. If it is a master suite, can the kids crouch down in the bathtub or in the rear of a closet, far from the door and wait until you say it is safe to come out? If they are old enough to be home alone, do they know about not telling anyone on the phone or at the door that they are home alone? What about calling 911? Preparation is the key to successfully defending yourself, your family, and your home.

Chapter 20

PROPORTIONAL RESPONSE

What is *proportional response*? It is meeting a threat with a similar, or lesser, level of response. A verbal assault may dictate an apology and a backing away to avoid escalating the situation. You might be right, and they are wrong, but be the bigger person, apologize and get away while you can! It is not always easy, but it is better to be humble and walk away than to stay and end up in a fight for your life.

My introduction to Proportional Response came when I was stationed in South Korea with the U.S. Air Force. I had been hiking in the hills beyond the base, alone (I know … now I know, anyway). I was approached by a local. He knew a little English and attempted to make a little small talk. I was used to that, as I often encountered Koreans who wanted to practice their English. It didn't set off any warnings for me as the Koreans I had met were generally very polite, respectful people. Eventually, he made it clear he was interested in more than talk. I said no and started to walk away. He grabbed me, and I hit him square in the chest with both hands, knocking him down and giving me a chance to run away. Later, I wrestled with myself. I had taken classes, I know lots of "moves" to defend myself. I should have been able to take him on, but instead all I did was knock him down and run. It was a couple days later that I spoke with a counselor who told me that I didn't do anything wrong, I did exactly what I was trained to do. I did just enough to get out of immediate danger, but I did not do anything to escalate the situation. That was a proportional response. It was just enough without escalating the situation beyond what it needed to be.

A gun is neither a good luck charm, nor is it always the right response. Many different circumstances will drive your level of response. Maybe the threat is not perceived to be inherently dangerous. Maybe you are in a crowded area and cannot safely deploy your firearm without jeopardizing innocent lives. Every situation is different. Your best defense is what is between your ears. Be alert, be aware, practice your *what if* scenarios, and stay safe!

Chapter 21

PRACTICE VERSUS DEFENSIVE SHOOTING

Practicing your shooting fundamentals is important. You need to learn and build muscle memory. Practice your aiming, your trigger control. Develop your accuracy. These things are important and will go a long way toward making your shooting practice more fun, and to helping you if you decide to carry for personal defense.

Once you have mastered the basics, you can begin to transition to the skills that are needed for effective personal defense. The fundamentals that you practiced in your early stages of learning have become safe habits and you have built the muscle memory to execute them effectively. Defensive shooting is a different mind-set. You will most likely not have time to think through your response, or to aim for a perfect group. In a defensive situation two shots in thirty seconds in a three-inch area will probably not be as effective at stopping the threat as three shots in a six-inch area within ten seconds.

As you progress in your skills, you can begin to make the transition from target practice to defensive practice. Practice your natural aim, which is less focus on your sights and more on the natural extension of your arm, hand, gun as a single unit, developing your instinctive aiming. You may not be able to assume your perfect stance, your perfect aim point. You may need to shoot one-handed, around a barrier, from a kneeling position, while lying on your back. You probably won't be able to practice all of these at the range you use. You can practice all of it at home with a blue gun, in a dry fire area, or even using an "air gun" where you use your hands in the shooting hold but your gun is imaginary. You can roll on the ground, practice being attacked. If you have a training partner, you can use a blue gun or an "air" gun and take turns being the defender.

Consider some advanced classes, such as the NRAs Personal Protection in the Home or Personal Protection Outside the Home. Look into a Combat Focused® Shooting (CFS) course, developed by Rob Pincus. Don't let the word "Combat" throw you. If you are in a defensive situation, you are in "Combat" mode. The skills you learn in a CFS class may save your life if you are ever confronted by a serious threat. CFS isn't really an advanced class; I recently completed a course and found that the instruction was geared to the students' level; we built on skills throughout the day. The students ranged from one who had never drawn from a holster to a law enforcement officer and every skill level between. By the end of the day I was tired but shooting better than ever and feeling more prepared for a defensive encounter.

Most important, practice for the real-world situations. Practice the skills you learn in the advanced classes. Sure, it is fine to go to the range and have fun, but a significant portion of your practice time should be challenging you to master new skills and improve on existing ones.

Chapter 22

IF ONLY

If Only, two small words, six letters, but you put them together and they carry so much weight. If only, words I hope I never have to use.

If only I had trusted my intuition …
If only I had not left my gun at home …
If only I had paid attention to my surroundings …

Powerful words, powerful sentiments.

Carrying a gun is a tremendous responsibility. You must hold yourself to a higher standard than the average citizen. You are prepared and ready to defend your life, and those of others if called to, but it will be because someone else made the decision for you. To carry a gun, you are choosing to respond, but also choosing not to initiate. You are accepting an awesome responsibility, and risks. You must be aware of your surroundings. You must be able to read what is happening and make a judgment in seconds, or less. Then, you must be able to articulate why you made the judgment you did. What clues did you see, what things did you sense, what actions tipped you off that there was trouble?

Using your gun to defend yourself will likely change your life. There may be legal consequences. There may be social consequences.

You may suffer emotionally. Some family and friends will see you as a hero; some may see you as an abomination.

Remember, you are important, your life is important; you have the right to defend yourself. You do not choose to initiate a confrontation but you choose to fight when someone else make the choice to start.

If only … words I hope you never have to use.

Chapter 23

NATIONAL TAKE YOUR DAUGHTER TO THE RANGE DAY

The third Saturday in June is National Take Your Daughter to the Range Day. The inaugural event was held June 9, 2012, and was a great success at ranges from coast to coast and in Hawaii with many girls and young women being introduced to shooting for the first time.

NTYDTTRD came about after reading world-champion shooter Julie Golob's book *Shoot*, in which she writes about how she grew up going to the range with her dad and then hearing from other women about going shooting with their parents and how much they enjoyed it. On Sunday, January 22, 2012, a Facebook page was created to solicit feedback for the idea and see if grassroots support could get it going. Just a few days later, on January 26, 2012, the page had already received 298 "likes." A nonprofit corporation was formed to oversee the event, and we were off and running.

Boys learn to shoot in Scouts or with their dads. Often, the girls are left behind because shooting is not viewed as girly. Well, women can and do shoot, and shoot well! Learning to shoot gives young women confidence, helps to build self-esteem, can provide a great sense of community, and introduces them to a sport they can participate in their whole lives.

I had previously assumed that most women came to shooting through a desire for self-defense, and I had not been aware of the fun and family aspects of the sport. However, after reading Julie Golob's book, I was inspired to start asking questions through my blog, *Female and Armed*, and I came to understand that women shoot for many different reasons and in many different capacities.

I have grown since I started shooting. I am more confident, it helped my sense of self-esteem to learn a new sport, and I know I can defend myself. More than that—it is fun! What could be better than a family bonding experience, a great experience for young girls, and maybe even introducing someone to a sport they can enjoy the rest of their lives?

I shared my thoughts with cofounder Evan Carson (also my firearms instructor), and the idea for a National Day was born.

NTYDTTRD is a great example of the positive power of social media. The idea was launched on Facebook, and then spread exponentially via reposts, blogs, and twitter. It was a positive idea whose time had come.

I hope you will consider getting involved in the future, hosting, sponsoring, participating or volunteering!

For more information about NTYDTTRD visit www.National-TakeYourDaughtertotheRangeDay.com.

Figure 23-1. National Take Your Daughter to the Range Day Logo

GLOSSARY OF TERMS———

Following are terms you are likely to come across in shopping, conversation, or class.

+P+	Refers to overpressurized ammunition that has additional power. Ensure that your firearm is rated to accept the additional pressure to avoid injury or damage to your firearm.
Action	The actions that are engaged when the trigger is pulled.
Air Gun	Using your hands to simulate holding a firearm, sometimes used for practicing stance or in self-defense practice with a partner.
Ammunition	The cartridges that are used in firearms, also called ammo and rounds.
Back Strap	The rear of the grip.
Blue Gun	An inert, nonfunctional, training gun.
Bore	This is the opening down the middle of the gun that the bullet travels through.
Bore Brush	A nylon or metal brush that is used to clean the bore of lead and debris. These are sized to fit your specific caliber of gun.

Bore Cleaner	This is a solvent that is used to clean lead and fouling from the inside of the gun.
Brandishing	Deliberately displaying your gun in an intimidating or threatening manner.
Brass	Slang term for the case that contains the primer, powder, and bullet. Commonly made from brass or aluminum.
Brass Dance	The gyrations that you go through when a piece of hot brass connects with your skin.
Bullet	The projectile that exits the muzzle when the gun is fired.
Caliber	The circumference of the ammunition or the inside of the bore.
Cartridge	The combined components of ammunition; primer, powder, and bullet.
Cartridge Case	The case that contains the primer, powder, and bullet.
Cleaning Brush	A toothbrush-like cleaning tool used to scrub debris from the exposed (after disassembly) part of the gun.
Cleaning Rod	A plastic or soft metal rod that cleaning tips attach to and that gently guides them down the bore of the gun.
Concealment	Shielding that hides you from view but does not provide a protective barrier, such as shrubbery.

Cover	Shielding that hides you from view and provides a protective barrier, such as a concrete wall.
Cylinder Release	The "button" that is pressed to release the cylinder on a revolver allowing it to open for loading, unloading, or cleaning.
Defensive Posture	The natural position the body assumes when startled, squared off toward the threat, hands up, alert.
Defensive Rounds	Ammunition that is primarily used for defensive shooting. Generally hollow point or frangible. These rounds have less risk of penetrating the target, walls, etc., in order to minimize the risk to innocents.
Desiccant	A drying chemical.
Dominant Eye	The eye that offers the most natural sight alignment.
Dominant Hand	The hand that is generally used for writing and most fine motor tasks.
Double / Single Action (DA/SA)	The number of functions performed by a trigger pull.
Double Action (DA)	Double Action cocks and releases the hammer.
Dry Fire	Practice fire in a safe, dedicated environment without ammunition or with snap caps or dummy rounds.

Dummy Round	An inert cartridge, with no primer or powder, a plastic tip. Used in dry fire practice to protect the firing pin or striker, or in malfunction drills. Sometimes called a snap cap.
Ears	Slang for hearing protection.
Ejector Rod	The rod on a revolver that is used to assist in expelling spent cartridges.
Eyes	Slang for eye protection.
Frame	The internal skeleton of a gun.
Front Sight	The post of the farthest end of the barrel that you use to sight the gun.
Front Strap	The front panel of the grip.
Grip	The portion of the gun that you wrap your hand(s) around to securely hold and fire the gun.
Grip Master	A hand strengthening tool that allows you to work fingers individually and comes in different resistance levels.
Gun Oil	A lubricant designed to reduce friction on moving gun parts.
Gun Safe	A protective locking container for gun(s).
Hammer	The mechanism that falls forward to impact the firing pin causing the gun to fire.
Hammer Spur	The tang, or tail, on the end of the hammer that allows you to manually cock the gun.

Hang Fire	A perceptible delay between pulling the trigger and the "bang."
Hollow Points	A type of ammunition that has an open nose and a soft covering around the bullet, designed to expand and lose most of their velocity upon impact.
Holster	The protective carrying holder for your gun.
Indexing	Aligning the index finger along the front of the magazine to ease insertion into the magazine well of your pistol.
Intent	The overt indicator of a threat.
Isosceles	A three point triangle.
IWB	Inside the Waist Band, as in an IWB Holster.
Jag	A cleaning tip that attaches to a cleaning rod and is used to push a path through the bore or barrel of your gun.
Kubaton	A metal or wooden dowel that can be used defensively.
Kydex	A thermoplastic acrylic that can be molded into a shape and is quite durable.
Mag Well	The opening in the grip where the magazine is inserted.
Magazine	The holder of ammunition for a semi-automatic.

Magazine Release	The button that disengages the magazine allowing it to fall from the magazine well.
Magnum	A higher power designation for ammunition.
Malfunction	A mechanical failure of the firearm.
Means	The reasonable ability to carry out a threat.
Misfeed	Failure of a round to feed into and align properly in the gun.
Misfire	When a round does not ignite and fire when the trigger is pulled (not distinguishable from a Hang Fire without waiting).
Muzzle	The business end of the gun.
Nondominant Hand	The opposite of the dominant hand.
NRA	National Rifle Association
Opportunity	The ability to carry out a threat; timing, space, and availability.
OWB	Outside the Waistband, as in a holster.
Owner's Manual	The primary reference for information about your firearm.
Patches	Fabric, generally cotton or linen, squares used for cleaning a gun. Sized by caliber.

Pepper Spray	Oleoresin Capsicum, a spray that is designed to irritate the eyes and mucous membranes, temporarily stopping an assailant.
Plinking	Shooting for fun at moveable or reactive targets.
Pocket Pistol	Slang for small, pocket-sized pistols.
Powder	The compound contained in a cartridge that builds up gas pressure as it burns until it propels the bullet out the end of the cartridge.
Practice Rounds	Ammunition designed for range shooting, generally with a rounded or blunt tip. Tends to be less expensive than defensive ammunition, but it shouldn't be used for defense as it is more likely to penetrate a target and continue on.
Primer	The chemical compound contained in the end of the cartridge case that burns, igniting the powder.
Racking the Slide	Pulling the slide back to chamber a round and prepare the gun to fire.
Range	A specialized facility designed for firearms practice.
Range Safety Officer	A specially trained and qualified safety officer who monitors and enforces the safety rules on the range.
Rear Sight	The sight at the rear end of the gun, usually a notch or "U" shape.

Recoil	The rise of the muzzle as a result of the bullet being propelled out of the gun.
Recoil Spring	The spring inside a semi-automatic pistol that propels the slide back to chamber a fresh round when the gun is fired.
Revolver	A pistol with a rotating cylinder.
Rounds	Also known as ammunition or cartridges.
Safe Direction	A direction that you point the gun where there will be no injury or property damage if the gun were to be fired.
Semi-Automatic	A pistol that uses a single chamber and barrel, with a mechanism powered by the previous shot to load a fresh cartridge into the chamber.
Shooting Platform	The stance, grip, and posture that make up the shooting stance.
Sight Alignment	The alignment of the pistol sights to the target.
Sight Picture	The image of the sights properly aligned on the target.
Sights	The post and notch on the gun that aid in alignment on the target.
Single Action (SA)	The trigger performs one function, releasing the hammer.

Slide Lock	The mechanical button the holds the slide in the rear/open position.
Slotted Tip	A cleaning tip that is attached to a cleaning rod to push patches through the bore. Similar to a needle eye.
Snap Cap	An inert cartridge, with no primer or powder, a plastic tip. Used in dry fire practice to protect the firing pin or striker, or in malfunction drills. Sometimes called a Dummy Round.
SOB	Small of the Back, as in a holster carried at the center of the back.
Squib	An ammunition malfunction indicated by a noticeably reduced recoil, sound, or feel. Often a result of reduced pressure from the powder burn.
Stance	The proper shooting posture.
Star Plate	The plate on the end of the ejector rod of a revolver that helps to release spent cartridges.
Stove Pipe	A malfunction where the spent casing is caught in the ejection port.
Strong Hand	Also known as the dominant hand.
Stun Gun	A device that administers a nonlethal electric shock on contact to temporarily incapacitate an attacker.

Taser	A device that administers a nonlethal electric shock, generally by release of prongs, to temporarily incapacitate an attacker.
Trigger	The "lever" that is pulled to release the hammer or striker and fire the gun.
Trigger Control	The steady, consistent squeeze of the trigger and subsequent release to the reset point.
Trigger Guard	The loop surrounding the trigger of a firearm and protecting it from accidental discharge.
Trigger Pull	The pounds of pressure required to pull the trigger back to cause the gun to fire.
Weak Hand	The nondominant hand.

ABOUT THE AUTHOR

Lynne Finch is a NRA Certified Instructor in Pistol, Personal Protection in the Home, Refuse to be a Victim, Home Firearms Safety, and a Certified Range Safety Officer. She is also a Certified Defensive Firearms Coach and a SABRERed Certified Pepper Spray instructor. She is an adjunct instructor with Innovative Defensive Solutions, LLC in Manassas, Virginia. Lynne is also the author of a popular blog, http://  www.FemaleandArmed.Blogspot.com, and runs the facebook page: Women Firearms Instructors.

In 2012 Lynne co-founded National Take Your Daughter to the Range Day, a nationwide annual event to promote gun safety and family bonding through the shooting sports. She is President of NTYDTTRD, Inc, a non-profit corporation that was founded to serve as an umbrella organization for the event. She authors a Facebook page for the event, National Take Your Daughter to the Range Day, as well as maintaining the website, http://www.NationalTake YourDaughtertotheRangeDay.com.

In 2012 she completed the Winchester NRA Marksmanship Program for Handguns, earning her Distinguished Expert medal. She is currently working on the Light Rifle program.

Lynne, who is originally from Iowa, spent 20 years in the United States Air Force, and retired in the Northern Virginia area where she worked as a government contractor for several years before joining the Federal workforce.

She resides in Northern Virginia with her husband Russ Charlesworth Jr., and their two adorable shelter cats, Rhiannon and Cinnia.

Shoot
Your Guide to Shooting and Competition

by Julie Golob

Foreword by Sandy Froman

Whether you're a firearms enthusiast, an experienced shooter, or someone who has never even held a gun, *Shoot: Your Guide to Shooting and Competition* will help you explore different types of firearms, understand crucial safety rules, and learn fundamental shooting skills. This book provides an introduction to a wide variety of shooting sports through detailed descriptions that relate each type of competition to everyday activities and interests. High-quality photography from actual competitions and step-by-step instructional images augment the clearly written descriptions of both basic and advanced shooting skills.

$16.95 Paperback • ISBN 978-1-61608-698-5

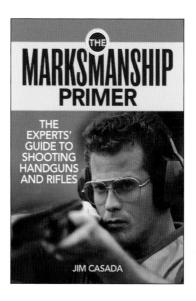

The Marksmanship Primer
The Experts' Guide to Shooting Handguns and Rifles
by Jim Casada

The Marksmanship Primer serves as a road map to greater shooting proficiency as well as greater enjoyment of the sport of shooting. Jim Casada, renowned outdoors author and editor, has brought together the best selections from America's great gun writers of yesterday and today. Marksmen of all levels of experience—beginners, pros, and hobbyists—can benefit from this collection of shooting wisdom.

Topics include:
- Positions for Rifle and Handgun Shooting
- Sighting In
- Ballistics
- Rifle Marksmanship for the Hunter
- Accuracy at All Distances
- Hunting with the Handgun
- Physical and Mental Fitness for the Marksman

$14.95 Paperback • ISBN 978-1-62087-367-0

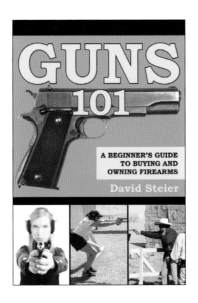

Guns 101

A Beginner's Guide to Buying and Owning Firearms

by David Steier

With a background in firearms instruction, sales, and organizations, Steier's knowledge has been cultivated through years of in-depth experience and personal dedication. In *Guns 101*, Steier covers the basics (what guns are for and how they work), but also discusses many types of firearms, firearm accessories, and gun activities—enough to help any reader carry on an intelligent conversation. From shop etiquette to do-it-yourself repairs, *Guns 101* answers all of your gun questions. Complete with diagrams and photographs that make all of the technical details clear, this book is essential reading for any newcomer to the world of guns.

$14.95 Paperback • ISBN 978-1-61608-287-1

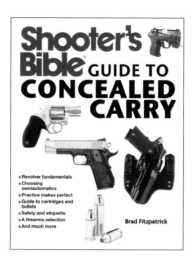

Shooter's Bible Guide to Concealed Carry
by Brad Fitzpatrick

Don't wait to be placed in a dangerous setting faced with an armed attacker. The *Shooter's Bible Guide to Concealed Carry* is an all-encompassing resource that not only offers vital gun terminology, but also suggests which gun is the right fit for you and how to efficiently use the device properly, be it in public or at home. Firearm expert Brad Fitzpatrick examines how to practice, how to correct mistakes, and how to safely challenge yourself when you have achieved basic skills. Included within is a comprehensive chart describing the various calibers for concealed carry, suitable instructions for maintaining it, and, most importantly, expert step-by-step instructions for shooting.

$19.95 Paperback • ISBN 978-1-62087-580-3